MANUFACTURERS VIDEO CONTENT GOLDMINE

UNEARTH THE HIDDEN OPPORTUNITIES

DAN BARKER

CONTACT DAN BARKER

dan@danbarkerstudios.com

For Poppy, Isabel, Rose, Frank, Patience and Jemima.

CONTENTS

PREFACE

There was once a farmer who'd heard of other farmers making their millions discovering diamond mines.

These stories got the farmer so excited that he could hardly wait to sell his farm and go prospecting for diamonds himself.

He spent the rest of his life searching for these diamond mines but had no success.

Sadly, the farmer found himself in poverty, having spent all the money from the sale of his farm trying to find diamonds.

Meanwhile, the man who'd bought his farm happened to be crossing a small stream on the property one day when a bright glimmer of colourful light caught his eye - it was coming from the bottom of the stream...

He reached into the water and picked up a stone. It was a fairly large stone, bright and beautiful. He held it up, admiring it as it glimmered against the sunlight. He took the stone home and placed it on the mantel over his fireplace as a decoration.

Several weeks later a friend came by to visit. The glimmering stone over the fireplace caught his eye and he picked it up to get a closer look.

As he felt the weight of the stone in his hands, he was in shock.

He said to his farmer friend, "This must be one of the largest diamonds ever discovered."

The farmer didn't believe him.

He told his friend that his creek was full of stones just like that one, not all as large as the one on the mantel, but the stones were sprinkled generously throughout the bottom of the stream right here on his property.

The farm the farmer had sold so he could find a diamond mine turned out to be one of the most productive diamond mines on the entire African continent.

The first farmer had owned - free and clear - acres of diamonds.

But he had sold them for practically nothing to look for them elsewhere.

(Story adapted from www.tyemple.edu and a summary by Dean Bokhari on www.meaningfulhq.com)

FOREWORD

As I say to many people I work with; manufacturing, media and the way people digest content has changed a lot over the last five years. No longer can you just churn out the same old content hoping to, just maybe, capture some attention.

With so much content available and so much competition, unless you do something different, you'll just blend in.

In this book, Dan explains the vast number of opportunities that video offers to your marketing mix, where to start and what goals to focus on. It is packed with ideas on the types of videos you could produce, from a simple short video filmed on your mobile, to a bigger production that showcases the difference you make to your customers' operations every day.

The latest data from the Content Marketing Institute shows that marketers still face challenges with content, and that video (both long and short form) is a big area of growth for many. Getting it right is so important and this book will help you set up the right foundations for success.

Enjoy reading this book, please be inspired and embrace what you learn from it. The opportunity to stand out with great content has never been stronger and you should consider how video can be part of your marketing mix now and in the future.

My challenge to you is this, how can video help you tell your message more effectively, how can video show why you're relevant to your targets, how can video build credibility to attract more attention from prospects that matter, or nurture the buyer journey of someone who already knows you?

I really think you'll find it a GREAT read.

Matt Chilton, founder of Zenoot.com

CHAPTER 1
INTRODUCTION

GETTING STARTED

We've all seen stunning videos of cool products, showcasing the latest tech innovations for your home or hobby. The sweeping lines of a gleaming product close up, gradually revealing itself from the dark and making us want to hand over our cash as quickly as possible!

You think about how you could make a video like that for your business - either your own business or the one you work in. Yes! Let's do some video marketing, let's make super-cool videos of our products or talk about our services. People will love it, they'll come flocking once we have a video!

But hang on. What we do every day isn't quite as cool as that. We're not building Formula 1 cars here! The same tasks happen day in, day out. Our products don't look like iPhones or swish tech toys. There's nothing to see here. How are we ever going to make a video about this stuff?

Generating ideas for video content in your business can seem impossible. This is something we hear often from prospective clients.

There is *always* something interesting to share. I promise.

When we sit down with marketing teams who don't have a clear idea of what type of video they'd like to make, the problem we have by the end of the discussion is which one of the video ideas we're going to start with!

This book brings together the advice I give on a regular basis. We're going to look at how to generate ideas for marketing videos from what you have right in front of you, today. Video content you can make for your business now, to help boost your leads.

You'll learn that your marketing content is actually helping people because you have something valuable to offer - the world needs you!

Helpful content buys people into your brand, builds trust with prospective customers and ultimately leads to the sale.

Video content is integral to all aspects of your marketing campaigns. Once you have videos in your toolbox, you have assets you can use across your whole business. Assets you can draw on for your next PPC (Pay Per Click) campaign, email newsletter, social media post, website, webinar, training day, staff meeting...the list goes on.

You probably already know that. But you might not be clear on where to start; and how to generate ideas for videos that form valuable assets.

We'll run through all the common reasons for not getting started. We'll address those excuses and by the end of the chapter, you'll be raring to go!

We have a set of principles to follow when thinking about content marketing. If you follow these, you'll build a solid brand reputation and people will look forward to hearing from you.

I'll then give you ways to generate ideas for more content than you ever thought possible. I'll help you see your business in a new light and the ideas will flow. We'll discuss quick social media videos and the more polished, high-production-value video assets you'd commission a video production company to make for you.

If you're feeling ready to start but just don't know what to make content about, how to do it or why you're doing it, block out your calendar for the next couple of hours, read this book and you'll soon be a content-generating, lead-producing machine!

HOW TO USE THIS BOOK

This book is designed to be a practical guide, with adequate space in the borders so you can make notes as you go along.

There's a detailed table of contents so you can easily jump to sections when you need to come back and remind yourself of certain things. Chapter summaries are there as a quick reference in the future, and to consolidate what you've learned as you go along.

I'd recommend reading the whole book to begin with, then coming back and jumping to specific chapters as needed. You may need a confidence boost, in which case chapters 1 and 2 will help, or you may want to reference some of the ideas for the types of video you can create, so chapters 5 & 7 will be of most use.

There are content generator bullet points at the end of the sub-sections of Chapters 5 & 7. Jump to these if you need prompts to help brainstorm ideas for your video marketing content.

However you use this book, I hope it provides the inspiration, motivation and information you need to create quality video marketing content to help propel your business forward.

WHY ME, WHY NOW

So, who am I and why did I think I could write a book about generating content ideas for your manufacturing business?

A degree in mechanical engineering led to my first job at Marshall Aerospace in Cambridge. I got into a specialism that, looking back, wasn't quite right for me. I could do it (static stress and fatigue & damage tolerance analysis), but it wasn't driving me - I was never enthusiastic about it. I loved aeroplanes from a young age, so on paper, it seemed ideal.

Although I never really enjoyed my work in engineering, I stuck at it for quite a long time. I had always wanted to run my own business but could never figure out what I wanted to do.

When it came time to make a change, I still wasn't in a position to start my own thing and opted for a location change instead; moving down to Bristol to work as a Fatigue and Damage Tolerance engineer at Airbus. I've always been pretty good at applying myself to what I do, whether I want to do it or not, and I soon achieved signatory level at Airbus.

I'm convinced the school system teaches us to put up with doing things we don't want to do for long periods of time! But I don't mean to blame anyone for my decisions - we all make choices every day and our situation is a product of all the decisions we've ever made.

Not long into my job at Airbus, I met a young lady at a party. She was beautiful, inspiring, and entrepreneurial, running her own business - a high-end boutique on the Herefordshire-Worcestershire border. When we got married just over a year later, I moved up to the area and decided to take a contract role with Safran Landing Systems near Cheltenham. This was intended as a way of dipping my toes into the world of self-employment.

After a strong start, the effects of the 2008 recession caught up and the boutique began to struggle financially. I had no experience running a business but tried to help as best I could. We decided to have a website built, thinking it would save the day by opening us up to a national audience. But as you probably know, simply building a website does not mean people will find it and it's a whole new thing to look after – almost a second business.

To our delight, our first baby, Isabel Joy arrived around this time too. We tried very hard to make the new website work (5am starts to upload products before going to my engineering job and doing the same at the other end of the day), while my wife, Poppy, was running the business and looking after our new baby daughter. But it wasn't enough. After leaving my engineering role for a few months and moving in with my in-laws to cut costs in a last-ditch effort to save the business, we eventually took the tough decision to close it down.

We were left with a large debt. We could have opted for bankruptcy, but we felt it was right to pay it all off. I went back to my engineering work, and we made a start.

During the website build and launch, I decided I might like to take the product photos for the website and bought a second-hand camera to do so. We enlisted the help of a professional photographer friend, and I spent days and days photographing and editing pictures of clothes for the website. I realised during this time that I really quite enjoyed taking pictures, and as such, practised a lot -

reading up, and listening to anyone who'd help me learn more.

Just after we closed the business, our local wine shop was also having a website built. They knew they had to photograph hundreds of bottles of wine but had no idea where to start. So, I volunteered to have a go.

I asked for advice and read up on bottle photography (quite a difficult process due to the reflectivity of the glass bottles), then went in and had a go. I managed to produce some fairly decent pictures - certainly good enough to get their website going. We agreed on a price and suddenly I was making a little bit of extra income from photography. For the first time since running a mobile disco when I was 17 with my mate Jim (that's another story!), I was earning money from doing something I enjoyed.

However, we had around £90,000 to pay off, so I had to stay committed to the engineering work. We worked through that debt and 3 years later we were back in the black. During that time, I'd become obsessed with photography and business. I knew I wanted to do my own thing one day and this looked like it could be it.

I spent any free time I had learning as much as I could, both about photography and business. Podcasts were extremely helpful, as they enabled me to learn on the go, whilst commuting to work, and at lunchtime - and occasionally, if I had a particularly tedious freeze-fit bush to analyse, at my desk (don't tell anyone!).

Over time, I began to pick up more photography work. I'd post it to Instagram, and later LinkedIn, showing what I was doing and talking about the process. I'd get involved in conversations on social media and start to meet people as a result, building my network and beginning to become known as a photographer.

Once I got into LinkedIn properly, I began to really enjoy the platform and was soon making more and more connections, through helping people, sharing behind the scenes, and having conversations. What I was doing was content marketing.

There are two significant points from those times. The first was about a year before leaving my engineering job to go full-time with photography. The owner of a web design agency I had got to know through Instagram, Harry O'Connor, asked if I'd consider doing video. He liked my photography work and saw how I could apply those skills to video, which he was finding very impactful for websites. I didn't have the time or resources to buy all the kit and learn everything to make video on my own. But I did know someone, a family friend of my wife, who was starting to make video.

We teamed up and made our first homepage video for Harry's business, VoodooChilli. It was a great success and what I loved about the process was the planning and scripting – developing the concepts to help bring it all together as a story that flowed well. With that video, I ran a small Instagram campaign offering to make videos for local businesses at a reduced rate, to build our portfolio. We had a few takers and created some fantastic work.

The second significant moment was when I posted a question on LinkedIn, asking about any struggles people had when commissioning commercial photography. A man named Jon Johnson answered my question - as it turned out, this was a very rare case of him posting on LinkedIn at that time! He told me he'd had problems when having engineering applications photographed, as the photographer hadn't really 'got' the product and as a result, the photos just weren't working.

Jon very generously offered to have a phone call with me - I'm now good friends with him 5 years later and know that generosity is a big part of his nature and hence, his business success. We discussed his comments in more detail, and it got me thinking - as an engineer and photographer, I could probably add some value here.

This was the start of pursuing my niche as an industrial photographer, and now industrial video production company. Although I resisted the idea of niching for a while (that's a whole other book one day!) it's been the best decision ever for my business.

The video side continued to grow, and our business now serves large, global manufacturing businesses with high-end video production services. I've been fortunate to find very talented team members to join me and make fantastic video content. Our current head of video production, Tom Harkins, eats, sleeps and breathes video!

To date, all my marketing efforts have been through organic, unpaid content marketing on social media, email and our website. I'm currently running a PPC campaign on LinkedIn, following the same principles I outline in this book.

Although I don't think that organic content marketing is the only way to go, when I look back, I realise that what I've done is achieve a reasonable amount of success through content marketing. And what I do now with my team, is bring that experience to our clients.

Consultancy has become a big part of the service we offer. Many business owners or marketing executives know they'd like to produce video, but don't necessarily know what type of video they could make to suit their objectives, or indeed whether they have anything worth filming.

We've advised many businesses on this subject over the years, and I felt the time was right to gather this advice into a book. Our mission is to help elevate manufacturing businesses. We do this through creating engaging video (and photo) content. But we can't serve everyone - we're not the right fit for every business - so hopefully this book will help you, wherever you are, and however you choose to make your video.

CHAPTER 2
YOU CAN DO THIS

WHY WE NEED MARKETING

Firstly, let's think about *why* you're doing this. If we break business down to its simplest form, we need to: make a thing & sell the thing.

It's that simple.

When you start a business, you probably already know how to make the thing - whether that's a physical product, digital product, or a service. But selling the thing is where it gets difficult. To sell the thing, people need to know about you (and your thing).

Making people aware of what you offer is called Marketing.

Marketing takes various forms, but essentially it consists of putting out information to the world, to communicate what you make and sell. There are different ways to do this and when some people think of marketing, they associate it with sleazy, old-fashioned tactics, trying to coerce people into believing you and trick them into liking you. And sure, there are people who take this approach. But it doesn't really work anymore.

Seth Godin is a hugely influential marketing expert, educator and author of 20 bestselling books. He describes marketing as 'a generous act'. Why? Because you have a genuine offering that can help people. Marketing is informing them you exist and letting others know you can genuinely improve their lives and/or help build their business.

This is the type of marketing we're going to focus on in this book. The type of marketing where we generously help people, without expectation of an immediate return (think long-term).

I was recently shown a diagram by James Ashford, the entrepreneur and best-selling author. The diagram represented a business as a cylinder, where every business function is contained within that cylinder. Many people see marketing as a thin disc on top of the cylinder. Like the cherry on the cake, or a bonus thing that gets done when there's time. In this position, marketing can be forgotten when you're busy, easily being replaced with more urgent tasks.

However, he said marketing should be the central rod within that cylinder, one that runs all the way through the business from top to bottom. It should never be forgotten, never be dropped and everyone should be involved with it in some way.

After all, if no one knows you exist, no one will buy from you. And if no one buys from you, you simply don't have a business. Of course, things need to happen after the marketing to ensure the sale takes place and the customer receives the product or service they've been promised. But it all starts with marketing.

And that is what all this content is for. It's mission-critical to your business.

Here's the thing we hear from many of our manufacturing clients; "what we do is not all that interesting", "there's nothing worthy of showing on camera", "all we have is an office/factory/warehouse"...

This book will show you that actually, what you do *is* interesting. You do have things to talk about and your potential customers *do* want (and need) to hear from you. The people who buy from you now and in the future must, by definition, be interested in what you do, right?

Even the most "every day" service is interesting to the people who need that service. Let's take septic tank cleaning as an example.

How do you access my property? What equipment do you use? Where do you take it afterwards? How do you clean it? Do you need access to water or power? Do I need to be home? Will it disrupt my garden? Is it noisy? How far do you travel? How do I look after my tank in between visits? What products/services do you recommend to help with that?

The list goes on...

Potential customers are interested in these things. And by letting them have the answers to these questions, you're helping them and building their trust. Once you have their trust, it's very likely they'll buy from you.

A constant feed of information and helpful advice from your business means you're top of mind when people come to need whatever it is you offer. The important words are 'information and helpful advice'. A constant feed of advertising is not interesting to anyone. But useful content is.

Gary Vaynerchuk is a serial entrepreneur whose success, in large part, has been built on social media content. He says that every business should see itself as a media organisation. That means, every business should be putting out a constant feed of content.

Consistency is key. The mistake we all make sometimes is to put out a splurge of content for a couple of weeks, then nothing for several months.... then another load of content for a week or so and back to nothing. This is what happens when marketing is not seen as the important core element within the business. It gets forgotten.

It's time to make a change. The aim of this book is to show just how much you have available to share. People do want to hear from you. Because you know things they want to know.

When you start putting out helpful content on a regular basis, it becomes fun. It feels good to be genuinely helping people and seeing comments saying, 'thank you' and 'Wow, I didn't know that, I'm going to use this today'.

If you're receiving these sorts of comments, you know you're on the right track with your content marketing and you'll begin to see the results in terms of all-important sales.

And *that* is why we're doing this.

YOU ALREADY HAVE EVERYTHING YOU NEED

By looking at your business from a different perspective, you'll soon understand why people outside your industry would like to hear about it and see what goes on.

Perhaps what you do on a daily basis seems mundane, but I promise you there's marketing magic in it! For starters, if it was that boring and worthless, you wouldn't have any customers at all, right? People are interested in what you do by definition - they're already buying or using your product in some way.

Even the dullest of widgets will have some appeal to people. Either the people making the products that use the widgets or the end user. Imagine showing the end user what goes into making this widget they take for granted every day. *You* know there's a lot that goes into it because you're involved with it every day. You're constantly making decisions about how best to manufacture that part, where to source raw materials and how to optimise the process.

You have everything you need to get started with making effective video marketing content. You even have an entire video production facility in your pocket - your phone. Technically, you have the capability to make 100 videos today.

You may not think you're creative enough to generate ideas for 100 videos. I promise; you are! All you need are some prompts to get you thinking differently and to understand why you're doing this.

By the end of this book, you'll have a thousand ideas and making 100 videos will seem easy!

WHAT YOU DO IS FASCINATING

One of the things we love about our work as a production company is being invited into businesses to see behind the curtains; how things work and what goes on. Before specialising in industrial work, we got to spend the day in a barber shop. I loved seeing how the barbers worked and interacted with the customers; how they would take tactical toilet breaks to avoid having to cut that 4-year-old's hair!

Later, as I started working more in the industrial sector, I got to work inside a factory doing surface treatments. This was something I'd dealt with on paper as an aerospace engineer, but never seen in real life. I remember the client being concerned there was nothing worth photographing, but I was fascinated and couldn't stop taking pictures!

There are plenty of other examples; have you ever seen how abrasive belts are constructed and glued together? Do you know how paint is manufactured or how large compressors are assembled?

These are all things that happen every day within the facilities of our clients. To the people working there, these everyday things are not particularly noteworthy - they see the same processes going on and assume everyone must know about it.

But put yourself in the shoes of someone who's never seen what you do.

Imagine your first day there, learning how everything is made and how it goes together, why things are done in a certain way and the little tricks people use to make the process simpler. What were you interested in, what excited you and what questions did you have? How about when people come to visit your premises; what questions do they have, what are they interested in?

That's who you're talking to in the content you're going to create.

Everything you do and everything your colleagues know is interesting to someone. You get to see this stuff every day, but we don't. And we'd love to see it!

Extract and share what you know, and you'll have a wealth of content ideas right there.

It's just a case of unlocking the potential.

ADDING VALUE

The basic principle is that you must add value to your audience through your content. This is a concept that hasn't changed, and I can't see it changing any time soon.

Whilst trying to help with my wife's website, I bought a book - The Dummies Guide To SEO (Search Engine Optimisation). At the time of writing, that was about 11 years ago.

One part stood out to me; where they talked about making content on your website that was useful to people. That way, when searching for the answer to a question, they would come across your website and find themselves shopping on your online shop shortly afterwards. Easy!

The concept of creating useful information has stuck with me over the years. It makes complete sense, and we see it all the time. Think about the last time you had a question and searched online to find the answer.

Where did it take you? Probably to a website with a blog post or video that answers your question. And the chances are the website was selling something you might need.

When we land on a site we find helpful, it has two effects. We feel grateful to them for answering the question and it gives them some authority in our minds, about whatever subject we're looking into.

A recent example was when I was researching drones, qualifications, laws and restrictions. I came across a great article on a website answering my questions perfectly. The article was well-written, and they clearly knew their stuff. I noticed they provided the course I would need to take and I phoned for more information.

I looked around for other course providers and although I could have bought the course at another provider for less money, I still came back to this first website when it came to purchasing and completing the course. Why? Because they'd earned my trust with this article.

Another example was when we had the fortunate opportunity to build our own house. Without knowing where to start, I searched for 'how to design a house for a family'. I came across a blog post, and it really chimed with me. The writer clearly knew what they were talking about, and it all made a lot of sense.

Again, they built my trust. In this case, the article was on a house building website and they'd written it as a guest contributor. I looked up the author and found my way to their website. And guess what? This was the architect we commissioned to design our home.

So, what does adding value mean? My definition of adding value in the context of marketing (it's different at other stages of the buyer journey), is providing useful and helpful content to your audience. Content that answers questions and gives advice. This should be our main priority.

In doing so, we'll build trust and establish authority in our field. If our main objective is simply to help people by adding value to their lives, the other benefits will flow from there.

So many marketers think they just need to 'get out there' and shout about what they do. Some will try and trick people into signing up for something... just so they can tell them more about what they do.

Telling people about what you do is not interesting to them... yet.

Help them first, demonstrate your knowledge. Then if they want to know more, they'll come to you. They'll be far more likely to buy if you've helped them first.

Seth Godin talks about push vs. pull, and I really like this concept. You can imagine yourself pushing loads of content out there - "come and buy from us", "look at all the great features of our product", "we can do this for you". It's tiring for you and for the people hearing all this stuff. They'll be turned off by your messages, unfollow you, unsubscribe and never want to hear from you again.

Alternatively, imagine putting out all this super-helpful content, genuinely serving people, answering their questions and adding massive value to their lives. They can't wait to see your next post or read your latest email because they know they'll benefit from the information you share. They talk about you to their friends and colleagues, who also subscribe and want to hear from you.

You have an offering of course, but it's mentioned in passing. Once every so often you talk about what you can do for them, but it's gentle and they don't mind hearing it because you've already provided so much value. Then finally they're ready to buy the product or service you offer. They simply aren't going to go anywhere else - you're top of mind and always have been. You're the expert in your field. You might be more expensive than the alternatives, but they don't mind, they know you're worth it.

Through this process, you haven't had to convince them of anything by *pushing*. You've convinced them by demonstrating your knowledge and generosity.

I mentioned talking about what you have to offer every so often and we shouldn't overlook this. It's easy to hide behind all the content marketing and think 'I don't want people to think I'm selling to them, so I'll never make the ask'. This isn't what I'm advocating. You're putting all this value-adding content out there for a reason - you're trying to run a business by selling products or services.

It's fine to mention your offering from time to time. After all, you know it can genuinely help people, so why would you hide that away? The approach we're discussing here is the opposite of the old-school advertising methods of push, push, push. People became tired of that approach a long time ago. The modern way is give, give, give, ask.

Or, ideally, give, give, give, give, give, give, give, give, give, give, give, ask! The more you can give, the greater the trust.

WHICH MEDIUM IS BEST?

Firstly, a note on the types of content you can put out there. Running a video production company, you'd think I'd only advocate for video. But I'm not. In fact, I'm sitting here typing this book! I like written blog posts, love audio podcasts and make regular no-budget video content for my social media.

Video does hold some unique values - people get to see you on camera communicating a complex message in a relatively short space of time. For some, it's easier to speak than to type (one day I'll get this touch-typing thing sorted!). And some people simply prefer to consume video content, rather than read a blog post or listen to an audio podcast.

However, it's not as simple as 'you must do video'. Some people prefer to consume their information through the written word. I read non-fiction books most evenings and I love that format. I find it relatively easy to consume and remember the information from a book.

Sometimes if I'm looking for instructions, I prefer a written blog post with a few steps outlined because I can simply jump to those steps and see what I need to do. Other times, I need a video to help me do something because it's difficult to understand from text and diagrams alone.

And then there's the audio podcast. For me, the audio format is special - I can listen whilst doing something else (driving, gardening, exercising) - I only have to listen, I don't have to watch at the same time. We can share conversations, interviews, insights etc. very effectively through audio only.

We're going to focus on video in this book because I believe it's where we can have the biggest impact on our marketing mix and it's where people struggle the most if they've not yet had a go.

However, the approach to generating ideas for content and the types of content you can produce are applicable to other forms of marketing.

So, when you think about your content, don't feel you *have to* use a certain method or platform. As I tell people regularly, it's your business, you can do what you like.

Some people will tell you 'You have to use video', 'you have to post to 15 different social media channels every day', 'you have to write a blog post every week'. Rubbish. It's your business, do what you enjoy doing. Because if you enjoy doing it, it's more likely you'll do it. And if you do it consistently, it will lead to results.

Don't let the medium or the pressure to post to every platform become a barrier to getting your content out there.

TYPES OF VIDEO

There are two types of marketing video; there's high production value, polished and beautifully edited video. And there's the quick social media video.

What I mean by the quick social media video, is when you pick up your phone and talk to the camera, or you film something happening within your factory (a process, a delivery etc). These videos can be made very quickly and put out instantly. They can be edited using a phone app and they do the job. They communicate a message and get you known on your social media channels. The advantage is the speed you can make and share them. You wouldn't post these on your website, necessarily.

The polished, high-production value video asset is generally something you would commission an external agency to make unless you have professional video production capabilities in-house. These videos are well planned out and communicate a specific message. The shots are beautifully lit, the audio is crispy, and they present a polished look for your company or brand. These videos are cornerstone pieces of content, that would be used on your website, as well as social media. They might also be used in PPC campaigns. Examples would include company videos, product videos, client testimonial videos and case studies.

Both types of video have their place within your marketing. The quick social media videos keep you fresh in people's minds. The polished brand videos showcase your offering in the best possible light, and you might keep the same video live on your website or pinned to the top of your social media for several years.

In both cases, generating ideas for these videos can be difficult. I promise, you have a *ton* of content you can create, whether you turn that into a high-production value video asset, or a quick social media video.

CHAPTER SUMMARY

- Marketing is essential to every business and should be a core activity.
- The old-fashioned advertising style of marketing doesn't work anymore.
- We can *pull* customers towards our business by being helpful.
- You have the content and technical ability to create video content *now*.
- Every business is fascinating when viewed from the right perspective.
- We can and must add value to our audience.
- Adding value builds trust and trust creates customers.
- The medium doesn't matter - this approach works across all marketing materials.
- You can create quick social media videos and high-production value cornerstone video content.

CHAPTER 3
NO MORE EXCUSES

With practice, creating and putting out content will become second nature. You'll soon be doing something and think "I need to document this". You'll pick up your phone and hit record, you'll take a picture and write a post, or think to commission someone to come in and produce a video asset about the work you're doing.

As we've discussed previously, you need to do this both from a business perspective - producing marketing content - and simply because you're a generous person who shares your experience and knowledge with the world.

However, there are a *ton* of reasons - or excuses - for not getting started.

We're going to address the excuses I hear most often. I want to inspire you and your team to begin making regular marketing content because it will produce real results for your business.

CREATIVITY

First, a note on creativity. This can be a blocker for people. Telling yourself "I'm not creative" is a great excuse for not making marketing content.

Picasso said,

> "Every child is an artist. The problem is how to remain an artist once he or she grows up"

More generally, this means everyone is born creative.

I've found this to be true myself. I trained as a mechanical engineer and worked in aerospace engineering for 13 years. I knew it wasn't a creative job and I told myself I wasn't creative. However, as I learned more about the world of entrepreneurship, I began to realise the work I was doing did have a spark of creativity about it.

Problem-solving of any type is an act of creativity. In my old job, when given a problem or constraint, we had to come up with a way of analysing the component that would solve the problem. This is creativity.

Sure, it's not the same as sitting down with a blank canvas and creating a stunning watercolour painting from your mind's eye. But it is creativity. And I believe we all have it within us.

As I learned more about photography and practised, I gave myself permission to say I was creative. It took a while, but I got there. And now I have clients who come to me and my team *because* we're creative. That's quite a change from sitting in an engineering office on spreadsheets all day telling myself I'm not creative.

I believe the same is true for anyone - you are creative, and you have a spark of creativity in whatever you do. Nurture the spark and it will soon turn into a flame.

If you've started a business, this is an act of creativity. If you've found a new job you enjoy more than the previous one, you've been creative in making that change. If you've taken a picture on your phone, made a video or written some words, you're creative. If you've solved a problem - any problem - you've used creativity to do so. If you've worked out the best way to get to a holiday destination, which combination of flights, cars, hotels, and public transport to use, then you've been creative.

Give yourself permission to call yourself creative. I give you permission now - if that helps!

DON'T BE SELFISH

What do I do if I'm nervous or intimidated by sharing information, showing what we do or putting myself out there on social media?

Don't be Selfish.

This was the answer James Ashford gave one of our members when he joined as a guest on a mastermind call.

Your knowledge and experience are unique to you and the way you explain things will resonate with certain people. Getting your content out there is an act of generosity and if you're hiding behind the excuse of being too shy or uncertain of what you have to say, you're denying the world your expertise.

We'll talk in more detail about storytelling later but remember this for now - it doesn't matter how bland or boring *you* think your story is, to others it's fascinating. I promise. I've interviewed a lot of people on my podcast, as well as spoken with countless more and it's always (without exception) interesting to hear how people got to where they are.

While it sounds harsh to say Don't Be Selfish, this might be the motivation you need to get started.

BEING ON CAMERA

Having said all that, I totally understand why it's intimidating to be on camera and why you might not want to! The simple answer to 'How do I get started?' is this;

Start.

Make your first video with no expectation of publishing it. Talking to yourself on camera can feel very strange, and let's be honest, it is! It's not a normal thing for most of us. The first few times I did it, I felt the same. You hold the camera(phone) up to yourself, look into it, start talking and even in a completely empty room, you're wondering if anyone is watching you and what they're going to think!

Then you worry about hundreds of people seeing this and what they'll all think. Will it destroy my business if people see me looking like this? What if what I'm saying is totally wrong? I don't look anywhere near as good as everyone else who does this!

Your first few videos are going to be rubbish. Any big social media person you follow was also rubbish at the beginning! But they started and carried on. And this is the only way to tackle the problem - head-on, by starting.

We're going to talk more about the specifics of how to record a video of yourself later, but if this section has motivated you to have a go - just do it.

Hold the camera up to yourself and hit record. If you do this now, when you bring in a production team to make your high-quality video assets in the future, you'll already have experience in front of the camera.

I DON'T HAVE AN AUDIENCE

"But I don't have an audience". Another great excuse for not getting started. And a very simple one to address.

No one had an audience to begin with. So, start posting and your audience will grow. Even if you only have one follower on social media or one person in your email list - they want to hear from you. And if *they* want to hear from you, it's very likely others want to hear from you too.

Get started and don't let the low numbers put you off - it's quality over quantity anyway. You only need one engaged follower to turn into a customer.

REPEATING YOUR MESSAGE

Another reason I hear for not getting started is the belief that if you post the same message twice, your audience will get bored and leave. Therefore, people tell themselves they only have a handful of posts they can ever create.

Well, here's the thing; firstly, if someone is bored of hearing what you have to say after the first time, they're not your ideal customer. Let them go, carry on telling your story and wait for the people who really resonate with your message to find you.

Secondly, not everyone will see every post you put out there, so repeating your message is serving your audience. Finally, people need to hear your message multiple times for it to sink in.

Gary Vaynerchuk is clear that he only has a small number of core messages. He repeats these messages, so they get through to people. Presenting a message in two different ways helps your audience because not everyone will understand it the first way.

Look at personal development and business books as an example. As you read more, you begin to realise that many of the core messages are the same. Some of the teachings on personal development from hundreds, if not thousands of years ago, are still being taught in modern books today. But *how* they're explained by a certain author may resonate more than the previous times you've heard that message.

An example of this is the book Buy Back Your Time by Dan Martell. Dan is a serial tech entrepreneur, best-selling author, investor and high-level coach to SaaS businesses. He talks about the need for an administrative assistant and which tasks you can outsource to them, with a detailed and practical breakdown of how to do this. I love this book. But the message is not new. I've been told previously I could outsource certain tasks. I'd just never worked out how to do it and what to outsource. Dan takes this message and presents it differently. His explanation and practical advice resonated with me. I was finally able to put it into action.

And that's what *you* should remember when you're worried about repeating your message. You owe it to people to keep repeating it because they may not have understood it the first time. Even if they have understood it before, they need reminding. We have a million and one inputs to our minds each day. Your content will be seen, but it may be forgotten an hour later after they've dealt with a problem in the factory, had a management meeting, discussed a shopfloor project, and seen 500 more social media posts! Repeating your message the next day is helping me, thank you.

Stop telling yourself you can't repeat your message. You can and you should.

THEY'LL DO IT THEMSELVES

Showing behind the scenes of what you do and how you do it can make people think their potential customers will simply do it themselves.

Take what we do for example. In my social content, we try to give people all the information they need to go and make a video themselves. We even run training courses on how to make your own videos, where we take everyone through the entire process, step by step, giving away all our 'trade secrets'. And people have said to me "Won't they just go and do it themselves instead of booking you?".

The answer is yes and no. Yes, some people will make the videos themselves and not book us, but they probably wouldn't have booked us in the first place, so it's not a problem. By showing them how it's done, we've achieved two things; firstly, we've genuinely helped them. And that is always a good thing, you can't lose by helping and providing service to people.

Secondly, we've got them started with making their own videos. This means they'll soon start to see the benefits to their business. Potentially, they'll want to make more high-level videos in the future, which they may come to us for, seeing as we've demonstrated our knowledge and capabilities to them.

Now apply this logic to your own business. If you show people how things are done there's a chance they might do it themselves. But they're unlikely to have become a customer in the first place. They may also have a go, realise it's harder than it looks and come to you for support. The other, much larger group of people will see that you know what you're talking about and are the experts in your field. They never had any intention of doing it themselves, but they've been searching for someone who knows what they're talking about. You've demonstrated your expertise, been generous with your knowledge and now they trust you. You're the only choice in their mind.

The best marketers I've come across actually take this approach to the extreme and say "Give Everything Away".

Let's take an example of a personal trainer. They're making videos of entire exercise routines to try at home via their social media channels. It's easy to think no one will hire them, as everything is available online. Some people will try the routines at home and have some success.

But many others won't try to follow the videos. They'll think "Wow, if they're giving away all this information for free, I bet the 1-2-1 personal training sessions are amazing" and they'll book. Both groups of people will also talk about that personal trainer to their friends, encouraging them to check out the exercises and advice being offered. This grows their audience and improves their chances of gaining clients even further.

You simply can't be seen as the expert unless you share your knowledge.

You can tell people "We're the experts in our field" and "We're specialists with the knowledge to help you". But until you demonstrate that knowledge, no one is going to believe you.

Think about your own journey as a customer buying a product or service. Perhaps the last thing you bought. Before the purchase, did you consume any marketing content? How did that company approach their marketing, were they sharing information, or helping you in some way? How long did it take before you decided to buy?

Some customers will take a long time to decide on a purchase, so it's important to stay consistent with your content. It may be several years before someone decides to buy, so this isn't necessarily going to be a quick fix. I know with our own business that some people have been engaged with my content on LinkedIn or email newsletters for a very long time before they come to us for a video.

Maybe they didn't need a video before, or they were unsure of who to go with. Either way, the continuous output of useful, helpful content is often what pushes them into the decision to book with us. And it's worth noting that a lot of the time, we're the only production company they're going to for that video - they've seen our content, they know what we can do and they're not looking elsewhere.

STORYTELLING

Storytelling is a bit like creativity in my mind. "I'm no good at telling stories" is an easy thing to tell yourself in order to procrastinate.

My coach Vincent Pugliese is a fantastic storyteller. He can recall stories from his past in great detail and tells them in a way that draws you in right from the start. He leads you on a journey, giving you enough detail to imagine yourself being there, then hits you with the punchline and a message which resonates through the story he's just told. Both his books (Freelance to Freedom and The Wealth of Connection) are full of fantastic stories from his inspirational career – well worth a read.

But what is storytelling when it relates to marketing content?

At its most basic level, it doesn't need to be a long captivating story about a certain situation. It can simply be a statement of fact about something you've done, or even plan to do. For example: "Today I went to see one of my original clients who's been with me since I started my business".

This is a fact, but also informs your audience about part of your story - you were once getting started and have loyal clients who've been with you since the beginning. Your audience now sees how your success has grown from that point; maybe the same situation they're in now. It gives them hope and inspires them to carry on. It builds trust in you and at the same time (if you tag your client in), promotes your client as a loyal, supportive person.

Storytelling is essentially what you're doing every time you make a social media post. However short the post is, there's some degree of storytelling involved.

But the importance of your story – or that of your business – cannot be overstated. Imagine two very similar products, perhaps two bottles of bottles water. If we pour the water out into glasses, very few people will people be able to tell the difference. However, when the water is in the bottle, many people will have a preference.

This is because of the story we associate with the brand. It may be the advertising campaigns we've seen – associating it with lush mountains in the French Alps. Or it could be that we've had one type of water at a luxury hotel on holiday and it reminds us of that time. The packaging of another might communicate that it's the cheapest, and that may be our preference.

Either way, it's the story we've been told in one way or another, that will make us choose one bottle of water over the other, even though the product itself is extremely similar in taste and will give us the same level of hydration!

So, what can we learn from these bottles of water and how does it apply to our manufacturing business?

A product without a story is a commodity. A widget manufacturer without a story is a commodity. A freelance designer without a story is a commodity.

I think you get the idea. Our story and that of our business and people is one of the key factors that separates us from the competition. We must tell our story as much as possible, so people associate our brand with our story. This will help them choose us over the alternatives.

When we talk about storytelling, don't be put off. Just remember that what we mean is telling people (in any way you like) about what you do, what you've done or even what you plan to do. Your story is interesting to others and it's important to share it.

As well as being creative, you're also a storyteller now!

FOCUS ON ONE PLATFORM

Thinking you need to put content out on every available platform can prevent you from starting. I don't get annoyed easily, but one thing that can annoy me is when I'm talking to someone who can't get started because they haven't figured out their workflow for posting their content to 5 different platforms simultaneously yet.

The reason this annoys me so much is because *every* time this happens, it's because they've done some training with a marketing expert who's told them they should be posting to all these channels all the time. And why do they say this? Because they're not genuinely trying to help, they're actually trying to sell their services by pretending to help them. They think "I'll run this free workshop to show how generous I am, but secretly they'll see how difficult it is to do, and afterwards, they'll book me to do it because they can't manage it all".

The idea that you must post to every platform is rubbish. Start with one and optimise that.

How do you choose the platform to use? It needs to do two things; the platform should be somewhere your ideal clients are hanging out. And you have to enjoy it.

In my experience, the enjoyment part of it might come a little later. You generally enjoy things more when you're good at them. And getting good at something takes time. As you start creating content, you'll build up your contacts, you'll interact with them, and get to know people. Hopefully, you'll meet some of them in person or at least on a video call. And over time, you'll start to enjoy it. I promise.

So please, don't listen to those people telling you that you have to do it all from the outset. You don't. Look at the most successful people in this space and you'll see how they started with one channel. Gary Vaynerchuk started with YouTube; Seth Godin started by writing a daily blog. Sure, some of them expand onto other platforms and channels, but they started with one.

Choose one and focus on that.

HOW MUCH DO YOU WANT THIS?

When I have resistance to doing something I know I should do to push my business forward, one of the things I'll ask myself is 'How much do you want this?'.

Do you want this to work? Or are you happy where you are? Are you striving for the next level, or happy to coast?

If you're feeling resistance to creating marketing content, writing a blog post, email newsletter or getting in front of the camera, my question for you is: how much do you want this?

We all feel massive resistance to talking into a camera. But the evidence is there to show that if you do this consistently over a sustained period of time, it *will* make a difference to your business.

And if it makes a difference to your business, it makes a difference to your income and makes a difference to your life. More time with your family, less stress and fewer worries; more holidays, more time on your mountain bike or hiking with friends. Whatever improvements you're looking for in your life, whether as a business owner or employee, one of the ways you can make them is by improving your business.

And one of the ways you can do that is through marketing.

So, try and get over your worries, self-doubt or lack of confidence and think about what *you* want in life. If you want it badly enough, pick up that camera and start speaking to the world.

"Give everything you've got and within 3 years something good is going to happen" - Vincent Pugliese.

IT'S NOT PERFECT

One piece of advice I love comes from James Ashford (again!). He says you should actually be a little bit embarrassed when you post something, otherwise, you've taken too long over it.

Now, some points to remember with this advice. This relates to quick social media videos. Your company video should not be an embarrassment in any way!

But the point with the quick social videos is exactly that, they're quick. The reason James says this is because he values speed. Getting something out there straight after an event or ensuring you have content going out every day can be extremely valuable. And if you're fussing over the small details of perfection, you'll never do it.

Secondly, this doesn't necessarily mean hit record and hit send, however it looks. You can still have a few attempts if it's not right. But again, don't carry on fussing over it just to try and perfect a detail that really, in the grand scheme of things isn't going to matter that much. Get it to the point you're relatively happy, then post it. Your message is what counts.

STARTING IS MAGIC

Starting is the hardest part of doing anything. Once we get started, it's usually fairly easy to carry on.

One of the interesting things about starting is not only does it become easier, but it also helps you generate more ideas. Start a daily blog and as you're writing, you'll be generating ideas. Start making daily social media videos and you'll have more ideas as you record. In fact, as I'm writing this book, ideas keep popping into my head for more information I can include.

Furthermore, as you put your content out, people will begin to comment back and ask you questions. These questions can generate more content for you.

So don't overthink this stuff. Get started. Why not put the book down for 5 minutes and record a quick video of your-self talking about something you do in your business? You don't have to use it; you can even delete it straight away. But make something, now. Send it to me and I'll happily give you some feedback.

OK, once you've done that, we'll crack on with the rest of the book. But please feel free to stop and create content any time you feel like it. And if there are too many ideas for now, make a note of them for later. I like to use an app on my phone because I always have it with me. But do what works for you - a notepad in your back pocket works too!

CHAPTER SUMMARY

- Creating and putting out content will become second nature over time.
- You may think you're not creative, but I promise you are.
- Give yourself permission to call yourself creative.
- Don't be selfish – share your knowledge and experience with others.
- Your first few videos will likely be rubbish – but get started anyway.
- You will build an audience over time. Get started even if you have no followers.
- It's ok to repeat your core messages in different ways. They'll resonate with people at different times.
- If you show people what you do and how you do it, those who do it themselves were unlikely to be customers anyway.
- The benefits of demonstrating your expertise will far outweigh the perceived risks.
- Share your story – it's what separates you from the crowd.
- A product without a story is a commodity.
- If you feel resistance to making content, ask yourself "How much do you want this?"
- Your social posts don't have to be perfect every time – your message is what counts.
- Get started and ideas will flow. *Doing* is where the magic begins.
- Getting started is the hardest part, but only needs to be done once.

CHAPTER 4
PRINCIPLES FOR SUCCESS

A RISING TIDE

"A rising tide lifts all boats", a quote often attributed to John F Kennedy, means that if everyone around you is being elevated you will move up with them. But you can't just sit there and go along for the ride, you have to be proactive and help lift everyone else.

One way to do this is to promote and support others in your content, whether through written blog and social media posts or polished company videos. Promote others and help to lift them with recommendations, shout-outs and mentions.

People love to give a referral. There's something that feels good about this process. If we already have a level of trust with someone, then knowing they trust this other person means we can move forward with some certainty they'll do a good job. We feel comfortable knowing they've come from a trusted source.

The added bonus of promoting those around you (but certainly not the primary reason for doing it) is that the people you recommend will be extremely grateful for the shout-out and may well return the favour one day. They may re-post your content on their channels, thereby giving you some extra reach and promoting you to their network. However, I'd like to reiterate this is *not* the main reason for making content that promotes others.

Make sure you don't fall into the trap of promoting people just because you think they have a large audience you could benefit from. You'll appear fake and have entirely the opposite effect you'd hoped. We can all spot a post where a mention of someone with a large following has been shoehorned in there, in the hope of gaining some extra reach.

Only promote people you genuinely believe are offering a fantastic product or service; those you really trust. This is incredibly important because you're putting your reputation on the line by recommending them. If I contact someone and commission them for some work on the basis that you've recommended them and they deliver a poor service, it makes you look bad. In my mind, I associate their poor level of service with you. My trust in you begins to decrease and over time I may not want to work with you as a result.

On a side note, this doesn't just apply to recommending people through your content and posts, but also to good old-fashioned word-of-mouth referrals. Make sure you're recommending people you genuinely trust to deliver a great service because it reflects back on you. Also, remember that if you've been referred by someone else and commissioned for work as a result, you're not only working for the person paying the invoice but also for the person who referred you. Their reputation is on the line too.

So, promote the people around you; people you would genuinely recommend to others. Talk about how great they are. If you want to super-charge this process, you can even promote others in your industry - 'competitors'. Remember, when they have too much work or get enquiries that aren't suitable, they need someone to refer those to.

EVERYDAY CONSISTENCY

I talk about niching a lot because I really believe there are multiple benefits. One of these is knowing what to post on your website, social media, email newsletter etc. Once you know what to talk about, you begin to have consistency in your message.

Why is this important? We live in a world where there's information coming at us at the speed of light every day (literally). More information than we could possibly know what to do with. And as a business, we have to get through that clutter and be visible. One of the ways we do this is by having a consistent message.

Our audience knows what type of information to expect from us. They know which subject we talk about, and they come to us for that information or entertainment. As generalists, it's very difficult to know what to talk about, so our message becomes mixed. Some days we're talking about x, and others it's y. As a viewer, I don't know what I'm going to hear about, so I choose channels where I know I'll hear about a particular subject, one that I'm interested in.

Years ago, there were only 4 TV channels in this country (fewer before that, but I'm speaking from my own experience!). Those TV channels had a niche - their niche was the very fact they were a TV channel. This was clearly unique, being only one of four in the country. This was a good enough niche and the programs shown on each channel could afford to be varied.

However, as time went on, more channels started to appear. Channel 5 came along. We started to become aware of the types of programs, broadly speaking, we could expect on

BBC 1 compared to Channel 4. More and more channels started to come out; Dave for a certain type of comedy, BBC 4 for another type. News channels, travel channels, cooking channels. By that point there was already a lot more choice and to an extent, you could pick the type of thing you wanted to watch at any point. Channels now needed to have a niche, so people knew what they could expect. This is how they separated themselves from the crowd.

Now add into the mix the gazillions of social media channels - YouTube channels, Instagram feeds, on-demand TV channels, movie channels etc. It's a crowded place for people choosing what they want to watch. There's so much choice out there, so many subscriptions you could have.

As a business putting out content (and remember Gary Vaynerchuk's advice of viewing yourself as a media company), you're competing with *all* these channels. We need to be clear about the subjects we talk about, so people know what to expect when they 'tune in'. They need to feel confident they'll get to see something that interests them, as they commit time to you and your channel. Time that is precious to them.

You must deliver high-quality value-driven content within your area of expertise.

BRAND CONSISTENCY

Whilst we're on the subject, we should talk about consistency between platforms. Most notably between your social media and website. After having seen you on social media for a while, people will no doubt want to find out more by checking out your website. This shouldn't be a shock - they need to see what they're expecting. They've grown to trust you over on social media, they know what you're about, what you do and who you do it for. When they go to your website, it needs to reinforce the message.

You do this by ensuring your website speaks to the same audience as your social channels. The work you showcase on your website confirms you are indeed an expert in the field you've been discussing on social. The content you put here - your videos, blog posts, articles etc., are all in your niche. If people are coming to the website via your social channels, the website should, in my opinion, be the final confirmation before they decide to contact you.

Of course, the journey in the opposite direction needs to do the same. Some people will come to your website first. They'll check out your social media channels to confirm that you speak about the niche you claim to be the expert in. They're also looking to check you're active on social media and get more of a feel for the company through your social feeds.

Consistency builds trust. If people know what type of content to expect from you, they're trusting you to inform them about that subject each time they log on. If you change topic, they'll lose trust in you. We know how important it is to build trust with your audience. So don't let them down by going off-topic - stay in your lane and deliver the information they're expecting to see.

CYNICISM & NEGATIVITY

My recommendation is to avoid posting cynical and negative content. Personally, it really puts me off when I see a feed of cynicism or negativity. In the context of adding value to people, this is doing the opposite - it's making my day a little bit worse.

Maybe it's making me a little worried or angry towards someone or something. Either way, it's not going to improve my day and may even put me in a negative mindset.

Think about politicians for a moment. One of their tactics is to talk down about the other person, trying to make themselves look better by doing so. However, it usually has the opposite effect in the long run. If you talk badly of other people, we're sceptical of working with you because we know you might talk badly of us to others.

As a rule, don't produce negative or cynical content. It doesn't add value to people and could damage your reputation.

POSITIVITY & ENTHUSIASM

Enthusiasm is infectious. Think about someone you know who's enthusiastic about what they do. I bet you enjoy their company and love to hear about what they're up to. Enthusiastic people bring you along with them; they pull you into their world. You can't help but share their excitement.

I understand you might not feel enthusiastic about what you do at the moment, but we need to tap into the reasons you started working where you are. There must have been something that drew you into the job.

The great thing about this process is that it benefits your marketing content *and* your life! It's easy to get bogged down in the day-to-day work, seemingly moving from one task to the next. This is your opportunity to stop and think about why you're doing what you do; to reignite the passion you had for the work in the beginning and to share that enthusiasm with others.

We talked about avoiding negativity. Now we need to share positivity to counter this. Being positive isn't about putting a fake sheen on what you're saying. It's about genuinely finding things to be optimistic about.

Think about what you do every day and which elements you could be positive about. I try and practice gratitude for what I get to do each day. When you feel grateful, you can't feel negative emotions.

An example of this was when I was in my old job. I found it hard to turn up every day, beating myself up about the fact I 'had' to do it, making it very difficult to get up in the morning and walk through that door. At the time, we were paying off the large debt leftover from a business we had to close. I felt tied down to the job, as I needed to pay off this debt.

However, I came to realise it was my *choice* to be there every day. It was my choice to pay off the debt. I could have found another job or chosen to file for bankruptcy. But I was making a positive choice each day going to work to pay off the debt. This shift in thinking had a massive effect on my motivation and ability to do the work. I realised no one was forcing me to be there; I was doing it of my own accord.

It can be hard to accept, but we all make choices and have ended up doing what we're doing through our own decisions. You may feel you don't have a choice and you have to go to work, but actually, no one is making you.

When you start thinking about what you do in this way, you can find the positives in everything. As James Clear says in his book Cosmic Habits, change your thinking from "I have to do this" to "I get to do this". Your energy will change dramatically if you start thinking like this.

As a result, you'll not only find the positives, but you'll find the enthusiasm too. And when you're creating marketing content, that enthusiasm will shine through, pulling people in, raising their moods, and therefore helping everyone.

The law of attraction says you'll attract people who are similar to you. By creating positive and enthusiastic content, you'll attract others with a similar outlook - probably the type of people you want to be surrounded by.

You will add huge value to your audience with positivity and enthusiasm.

ESTABLISHING AUTHORITY

The outcome we're looking to achieve from creating and posting our content - whether through social media, blog posts, YouTube videos, books etc. - is to establish authority in our niche.

As discussed, we do this through generously sharing our knowledge and genuinely helping people. People will begin to view you as the expert in your field and when they come to needing your services, you'll be the obvious choice.

You probably follow people on social media who you view as experts. They've gained this status in your eyes through sharing their knowledge and providing value to you over time. As a result, when they recommend a particular product, you're more likely to buy that product. If they provide a service, when it comes to needing that service, you're far more likely to choose them.

Your aim is to become that person in your area of expertise. Whether you manufacture widgets or provide a consultancy service, I want you to become the go-to person for that.

You may feel intimated by the thought of establishing authority. But this isn't about being over-confident or faking it (until you make it), it's about genuinely sharing what you know, to help others.

You don't need to know everything; you just need to know a little more than the people you're helping.

CHAPTER SUMMARY

- Promote and support those around you – everyone will benefit.
- Be consistent in your message and themes so your audience knows what to expect from you.
- Your website should echo the messages on your social media and vice versa, so there are no surprises when people go from one to the other. Consistency creates trust.
- Cynicism and negativity should be avoided – it's not adding value to anyone.
- Enthusiasm is infectious. Show your enthusiasm for what you do and if you need to re-discover your enthusiasm, think about what brought you to your job in the first place.
- Be positive, and make sure you mean it.
- The law of attraction says you'll attract people similar to you.
- Your content should be helping to establish your authority in your niche, so you're seen as the experts and the obvious choice.

CHAPTER 5
THE GREAT APPROACH

I've combined my approach to making content into five key points, which happily spell out the word GREAT. These principles should be the very core of your approach while making content, informing you how to craft your message and helping you generate ideas.

Although this book is focused on video marketing content, these principles apply across the board - whether you're writing a blog post, a social media post, a book, making a company brand video or a behind-the-scenes social media video on your phone.

You can make GREAT content every time by doing some or all of the following:

GIVE - to your audience

RECORD - and document your journey/process

EDUCATE - your followers

ADD VALUE - at all times (hint: value comes in many different forms)

TARGET - your message towards your ideal customer and the outcome you want

Let's run through each of these in more detail.

GIVE

Always be giving.

This is a mindset to adopt in your marketing and your life in general.

The concept of giving can sometimes be misinterpreted. People hold on tight and say "I'm not giving anything away". But I believe the best content marketers out there give it all away. They know the more you give, the more you get.

Giving can sometimes be confused with giving away your services for free. This is not what we're talking about here. I'm not suggesting for one minute that you go out and offer your services for free. This is not what's meant by 'giving' in the context of marketing.

One of my all-time favourite business books is The Go-Giver by Bob Burg and John David Mann. Written as a fictional story and drawing on all the experiences of the authors, this book demonstrates how taking an approach of giving is the major cause of success. In general, the most successful people in life are the most generous. This has definitely been my experience when meeting people who've achieved success in business.

Spoiler alert: I don't want to ruin the book for you, but the last chapter and final principle really brings it all together. This is the law of reciprocity.

All this giving is fine, but at some point, you also need to receive. Their point is that it's ok to receive. We're sometimes taught 'it's better to give than to receive', but what they say is that you can't have one without the other. You can't breathe out constantly without breathing in. You must be open to receiving when the time comes.

Put in terms of your marketing, this means people will come to you and want to buy from you because of all this fantastic information you're giving.

If you have any doubts about this giving approach, have a read of their short book.

The thing to remember about giving in your marketing is simply that it's the opposite of taking. We talked earlier about pull vs push marketing, and that is what giving is all about. You're giving to your audience rather than trying to extract something from them.

An old-school advert telling your audience how great you are, how much they should trust you and that they should 'buy now' is an example of pushing, or taking. You're trying to 'grab' them and shove some information on them.

The giving approach, on the other hand, provides them with information or gives them something of real value to take away. Perhaps you're showing them how something works or demonstrating the different use cases for your products. Either way, you're giving information which will genuinely benefit them.

By taking (or should I say giving) this approach, you're setting yourself apart by demonstrating your expertise and showing why you can be trusted. You're not telling them they should trust you; you're giving something of yourself. You're creating that 'pull' effect, whereby people will want to come to you because you're the expert. Not only that, but you're clearly generous.

"If they give away that much information for free, imagine what they provide when you pay!". This is what people will think when you begin to give generously in your content.

What I love about this approach is that it takes a load of pressure off you. Thinking about how best to *give* to your audience is a lot easier than thinking about how best to *get* your message across. Give at all times and you literally can't go wrong.

Forget the sales approach of ABC - Always Be Closing. I say ABG - Always Be Giving!

Think of every piece of content you produce being a gift to your audience.

What can you give to your audience today, that would genuinely benefit them?

RECORD

Record - document your journey/process.

When we're working out what to write or what to say on camera, we can fall into the trap of trying to put a veneer on it. You know that feeling when you're trying to second guess what other people would want to hear? Or when you picture yourself as someone else, with a different audience and you start trying to sound like them.

The words don't come out properly and you sound fake. People can tell it's not you speaking your truth. This kind of content tends to flop.

You can't understand why it's gone nowhere, because you put something out there you thought was on trend.

The way to reframe it is to think about your content in terms of documenting your journey. You're not trying to preach to people about how to do things. And you're not trying to impress them with your extensive knowledge on the subject.

Just be yourself and document what you're doing each day. Your experience and knowledge will come through naturally when you do this, so there's no need to pretend to be anyone else.

This approach forces you to get down from the dangerous podium you may feel like you're on. Why dangerous? Because when you position yourself up there, without genuine experience to speak from, you know it's wobbly. You know if you say something incorrect, others are going to judge you. And you know you don't have the experience to back it up. You're constantly wondering whether someone will 'find you out'; the imposter syndrome is real - because you *are* being an imposter.

When you take the approach of simply documenting what you're doing, you don't mind if you make a mistake. No one will criticise you for making a mistake and if they do, you don't have to fake anything, you can simply thank them for pointing that out and learn from it. You can even turn the learning into a piece of content and tag that person on your next post, thanking them with genuine sincerity for their help and advice!

By taking this approach, you're genuinely speaking from experience; you're doing the things you're talking about. And it doesn't matter where you are on your journey, you have something interesting to talk about - I promise!

Even right at the beginning, when you're figuring out the basics and getting started, this will be helpful advice to someone. They'll see you as genuine and resonate with your content in a way that simply doesn't happen when you're trying to give advice you haven't 'lived' yet. And 'yet' is an important point here - you *will* get there; be patient and document your journey.

Authenticity is a word banded about in the world of social media and marketing quite regularly. Stepping down and simply documenting your process is exactly what is meant by being authentic. It can be a difficult one to work out - how do I sound authentic? What does it mean to be authentic?

Record and document your journey and you can't fail to be authentic. This is you, talking about what you know, in a sincere way.

EDUCATE

Educate your audience.

Your content should be designed to help people, and in doing so, demonstrate your expertise. One way to ensure you're doing this is to think in terms of educating. Take the approach of teaching your audience how to do something or showing them why you do things in a certain way.

Educating people not only helps cement your position as the authority in your space, it also demonstrates why your product or service is the premium option.

As with the general approach of giving, one of the push-backs I hear often is that people are afraid of explaining how they do things, on the basis that people might do it them-selves. As we've discussed already, people who do it them-selves are not your ideal customers. They'll do it themselves regardless of whether you teach them or not. If *you* don't teach them, they'll go elsewhere to find out how to do it and then you really have lost your chance of converting them into a customer one day.

By educating your audience, you're showing your ideal customers why they should choose you *and* you're helping those who can't afford you to get started. One day they might get to the stage of being able to pay for your premium products or services.

The benefit you'll see in terms of gaining more customers far outweighs the risk of losing customers who might do it themselves. The risk-benefit analysis is heavily stacked in your favour!

Think about which aspects of your business you could educate people in.

ADD VALUE

Add value to your audience at all times.

Adding value covers all the things we've been discussing so far, and more. It's a term that's talked about a lot and sometimes it can be difficult to define.

To me, adding value can take many different forms. When someone comes to your offices, you're adding value simply by being polite and offering a drink. When someone phones, you're adding value to their day by asking how they are or enquiring about their family (assuming you know them).

With your content, you can add value in several ways. Think about it like this; in terms of social media content, what value are you adding to people who take the time to stop scrolling and watch your video? They should be rewarded for doing so.

This could take the form of giving some advice (give), showing them behind the scenes of what you do (record) or teaching them how to do something (educate). It could be that your video is entertaining in some way - does it make them laugh or think about something from a different perspective? I know the people in my network who make me laugh on their social media content and I'll take the time to watch their videos. They've added something to my day by entertaining me.

Critically, they've also helped cement their position as experts in my eyes.

In your cornerstone video marketing assets, such as your company/brand video, making a very high-quality, cinematic film with a great narrative and stunning footage will add value to your audience. You're rewarding them for taking the time to watch your video by giving them something entertaining.

As a side note on adding value, I've alluded to the fact you can add value to people in everything you do. Personally, before any meeting (with potential customers, employees, mastermind meetings etc.), before a photo/video shoot or a catch-up with new or old contacts from LinkedIn, my intention is always to add value in some way.

I don't think you can go wrong by taking this approach. And I believe that what goes around comes around. If you can always add value to people, even if that means advising them not to work with you, do it themselves or (dun, dun dah!) go to one of your competitors, that value will come back around in multiples.

Now for the tough love bit. Have a look back over the last few pieces of content you published and ask yourself whether you genuinely added value to your audience. Be honest - would anyone really care about those posts? Would they stop scrolling or take 3 minutes out of their day to watch your company video?

People are giving you their time when they stop to watch your content. That's not a small thing; time is our most precious asset. We don't want to waste our time or theirs.

By always adding value, I believe you'll attract many more people who'll convert into customers over time

TARGET

Audience

Before getting started you need to know who you're talking to when you produce all this content. You'll use this when designing your messaging and when you talk on camera – imagining yourself talking directly to this person.

As a business, you should already know the type of customer you're targeting. This will make all your efforts much more effective.

Niching and being specific about your customers is in my opinion (and experience) the best way to create a successful business. This is a whole subject we won't go into now (there might be another book one day!), but if you don't have a niche, I suggest thinking about it very seriously and working out what yours should be.

I understand why people are worried about having a niche. It can feel like you're reducing your number of potential customers. I was very resistant to niching at first, but once I'd done it, I only wished I'd have committed sooner.

Having a niche is the first step towards working out who you're talking to when you make your content. It's very difficult to decide who you're talking to without one - should I choose this industry, that type of business, this role within a business, that size of business etc? Once you have a niche defined, this process becomes far easier.

My friend Jon Johnson is very good at this and it's one of the very first steps he asks his clients to take when he's consulting - define who you're talking to.

Since committing to my niche of industrial, I've known the type of business I'm aiming to serve. And that has been a *huge* benefit. Before that, I struggled to know what type of work to show on my website and social media, what type of blog posts to write, who to connect with on LinkedIn and where to focus my efforts. Committing to the niche changed all this overnight. I knew what to post, who to connect with, where to invest etc. It was transformational.

To do this properly, create a fictional character (probably based on a real person to some degree) and talk to this person when writing social or blog posts, making videos etc.

To define who you're talking to, think about some of these things (not all will apply to you):

- What type of company do they work in/run?
- What age are they?
- Are they male or female?
- What's their job role?
- What are their struggles and challenges?
- What are they trying to achieve?
- What do they need from you?
- Are they married?
- Do they have kids?
- Do they have hobbies and interests?
- Finally - give them a name.

The more specific you are, the better. Some of the specifics (like age, gender, marital status) may seem like very granular detail, but 'knowing' these things will give you confidence when speaking on camera or scripting your videos.

When you're creating your marketing content, imagine talking to this person directly.

Outcome

There's no point in creating all this marketing content if we don't have a specific goal in mind. Of course, we're being super-generous with the content we post and we're helping our prospective customers build trust with us.

Having a goal might seem quite simple and some of you will say 'Well, our goal is obvious'. And it may well be - perhaps you want people to buy a particular product, or you know which service you want them to sign up to.

However, it can be easy to forget what specific action we want people to take towards working with us.

For example, if you provide a range of services, you may split your messages so you're talking about different services at different times. In this case, your audience could become confused about which service you offer and how to proceed.

A better strategy would be to drive your content towards one of your services only. This could be your entry-level service which gets them onto a journey towards your premium services, or it could be your top-level package straight away. Either way, they should be clear on what you're offering, so they know how to take the first step towards working with you.

The other aspect of 'target' is to know where and how you're going to use your video/content. This is more relevant to your high-production value video assets because, with the quick social media videos, it's obvious where you're going to use them. But the style of the video and your message will change depending on which platform you're posting to (LinkedIn will be different to TikTok for example).

We'll cover this in detail later when we look at some of the different video assets you can create for your business.

The outcome you want from your video marketing content should be well-defined so the video can be tailored to that message. Whether you want people to take a certain action or you're making them aware of a particular service you offer, make sure your videos (or at least the copy that goes with them) are pointing people towards this outcome.

CHAPTER SUMMARY

- Always be giving – it's a mindset.
- Giving does not mean you should give things away for free, it means ensuring you're providing something of value to your audience.
- Every piece of content you produce should be a genuine gift to your audience.
- Think in terms of documenting your journey/process – you don't have to know it all – be authentic.
- Educate your audience on what you do and how you do it. This will help establish your authority and demonstrate your expertise.
- Add value to your audience at all times – value can come in many different forms.
- They need to know they'll get value when they give their time to watching your videos. Time is our most precious asset, so we mustn't waste theirs or ours.
- Target – know who your ideal customer is and what the aim of the content is.
- Define your ideal customer down to a granular level, then you'll know who you're speaking to.
- Be clear on what action you want people to take – an entry level product/service, a free download etc.

CHAPTER 6
HOW TO GENERATE GREAT SOCIAL MEDIA CONTENT

I n this chapter, I'm going to provide practical tips for generating content from what you have in front of you today.

Your content ideas should always follow the GREAT principles we discussed in the last chapter. We're going to get specific and help you come up with a never-ending list of content ideas for your business.

It's time to open your mind and let the ideas flow! Give yourself permission to brain-dump *everything*. No matter how silly it seems, get it down and out of your head.

We discussed creativity earlier - you *are* creative, and you *can* think of ideas. Remember that getting started is the key here - you'll generate more ideas once you start, I promise.

We'll end each section with Content Generator bullet points. Use these as prompts to help your brainstorming session and get you thinking about what's possible.

I recommend you stop reading after each section and reflect on how that type of content could be relevant to your business. Grab a piece of paper, a whiteboard or open an app, and write down everything that comes to mind after having read that section and the Content Generator bullet points.

OK, let's get stuck in.

BEHIND THE SCENES

People love to see behind the scenes (BTS) of anything - how are things made, how they do that, and what goes into this process. Behind-the-scenes posts have consistently been one of my most popular types of social posts over the years.

This approach allows you to demonstrate your expertise, whilst adding value by showing how something is done or how things work. An example from my own experience is when I show behind the scenes of a photo or video shoot. I'll explain how the lighting is set up to achieve the look we want. These posts always go down well because I'm providing a peek behind the curtains!

During a podcast interview once, I was asked to talk about the process of a photo shoot. It was a video podcast, so I was able to share my screen. I showed all the photos I'd taken during a particular shoot, and talked through the lighting and what I was trying to achieve. To me, this process was my every day, something I'd been doing for years and almost took for granted. But I realised from the reaction of the hosts that this kind of insight was super-interesting if you've never seen it before. All industries have processes, skills and techniques which most people aren't aware of - until you show them.

Getting into the mindset of posting behind the scenes is a great way to generate content. Of course, there's a place for the more polished content - the company video, product launch video etc. But these can be accompanied by some behind-the-scenes content.

If people are seeing your company video for example, or a lovely high-production value video of an event and you also show some BTS footage or pictures, it feels like you're getting a privileged view into this secret world that others haven't seen. It feels as if other people have only seen the final marketing video and you're getting to see how it was made.

BTS content allows you to show more personality too. Although I would always suggest your official marketing videos need to have personality, you can afford to add more into the BTS footage. People being themselves, having the same struggles and difficulties as everyone else, and maybe having fun (if it's appropriate).

This helps people buy into your brand and feel part of what you're doing; again, building that all-important trust factor.

Content Generator:

- Get into the habit of pulling your phone or camera out at every opportunity
- Show people into your world
- What goes on?
- Who does what?
- Where are you today?
- Make sure you're adding value to your audience
- How are things done?
- Who can you promote or tag when you post?
- What information can you share?
- What value can you give?

MAKE IT PERSONAL

Everyone has a story. You might not think yours is noteworthy, but I promise it is. Telling your story and the story of your colleagues or employees is a great way to generate content. It engages people on a personal level. If I know you well as a person, there's a much higher chance I'm going to buy from you.

Don't shy away from talking about your personal journey, people love to hear about how you got there. You'll inspire some people as well, which is always a good thing. Remember, enthusiasm is contagious.

You're also the only person in the world with that story – you own it, and no one can copy it or take it away from you. You have a monopoly on your story.

Whether you run the business or work as an employee, there's a reason you're here and that's because you chose to be here - you made choices which have brought you to this business and this role. Tell us about those choices, why you wanted to get here and how it's positively affected your life. Encourage others to make positive choices.

As with everything, you can repeat elements of your story regularly to make sure people know what you've done and where you've come from. I mention my past aerospace engineering career regularly. It's part of my story and whatever you've done in the past is part of yours. Let us know about it so we can get to know you better and we'll no doubt want to buy from you.

Content Generator:

- Where are you from?
- How did you get into business?
- Why did you get into business?
- Where did you work before this?
- What are your interests outside of work?
- What do you love about your work?
- Who has inspired you during your career?
- Where did you study or learn your craft?
- Are there any qualifications you have or need?
- What are your future ambitions?
- Where is your business heading?
- Who do you like working with?
- What were the major turning points in your life that got you where you are today?

BUSINESS AND EMPLOYEE STORIES

As well as your personal story, there's also the story of your business - whether you're the owner or an employee. Every business has a history; it was started by someone, at some time, for some reason. Perhaps the founder saw an opportunity or maybe they were solving a personal problem and realised it would help others. They might have been working for someone else and decided to have a go themselves for some reason.

There will have been significant events throughout the history of the business. During a recession, for example, did the owners have to make changes or pivot their offering? Perhaps they had to move premises at certain times for interesting reasons. One of our clients was forced out of their premises twice under compulsory purchase schemes.

The individual stories of people working within the business are also fascinating. As with telling your own story, the same applies to telling the stories of other people. They may have a real passion for the industry or come to the business for a particular reason.

When it comes to other people's stories, you'll be surprised what you learn when you start asking. It's easy to assume you know everything about how someone came to work there but dig a little deeper; ask them about it, get interested in them and they'll usually be happy to share their journey with you.

Everyone wants to be heard. Give your colleagues an opportunity to talk about themselves and where they've come from. They may be hesitant at first, but I think they'll thank you in the long run.

As with all content you produce, it's important to remember to add value to your audience. Sharing the story of the business and its employees could easily sound self-indulgent and all about you.

But providing inspiring stories is a great approach to take; telling stories of the business and the people working there with the intention of inspiring other people to follow their passions or learn a new craft. Think about your audience and what they're getting from hearing these stories.

Content Generator:

- When did the business start?
- Who started the business?
- Why did they start the business?
- Where was it located to begin with?
- Were there some significant moments in its history - moving premises or times of struggle?
- Who works in the business now?
- Why did they join the company?
- What were they doing before?
- What experience do they bring to the company?
- What do they love about their work?
- What do they enjoy doing outside of work?
- How can you inspire people with these stories?

YOUR INTERESTS

It's easy to fall into the trap of seeing what's being posted by others and thinking you have to talk about the same topics. Being 'on trend' seems appealing because you see all your connections posting about that subject and getting a load of likes and comments. But I'd urge you to be honest with yourself and check whether that on-trend subject is something you're passionate about.

We talk about the word 'authenticity'. Although I think the word is over-used and can start to lose its meaning, the intention is to be talking about things in an honest, genuine and real way. If you talk about a subject just because it's on trend but it's not something you're genuinely passionate or knowledgeable about, it will be obvious to people.

They'll know, even if it's subconsciously, that you're not being real, and it will discredit you in a small way each time you do it. You'll also feel slightly empty from having done this - in fact, that may be how you'll know you've done it. You get that kind of flat feeling from it. You're forcing it out and sounding like everyone else.

Sounding like everyone else can seem tempting, especially at the beginning when you're starting out. But it will come through; we'll know you're doing it. Stop and be honest with yourself - are you really interested in what you're talking about? Or are you just talking about it because other people are?

People I speak with sometimes worry that talking about things they're passionate about, rather than what's on trend, might be a bad move because not many people are into those things.

Which post do you think will have the most effect - one where you're talking about something just to try and fit in with everyone else, or one where you're speaking truth about a subject you care about?

Besides, how many people do you *need* it to resonate with?

If you're into running, talk about running - turn your real-life genuine experiences from running into posts about your work and how the two are interlinked. If you're into knitting, tell us about it, let us know about the real you, what you're into and how passionate you are about it.

A Voiceover artist who contacts me regularly to stay top of mind once sent me a crocheted bookmark as a gift. In a handwritten letter, she explained how she was passionate about crochet and had made this for me. Although it's unrelated to voiceover or video, I understood a little more about her, which in turn keeps her top of mind even more. As a side note, this kind of thing also means people will talk about you to others - I told multiple people about this, and I'm telling you now!

By talking about your interests, we'll get to know more about you as a person, build trust and be more likely to want to buy from you as a result. No matter how niche you think your interests and passions are, talk about them.

My friend Dave Bird is excellent at this. He's passionate about Bob Dylan. He posts regularly about a topic and relates it back to a Bob Dylan song. Does it matter that you're not into Bob Dylan? No, it's the enthusiasm that comes through, whether you're a Bob Dylan fan or not. Dave's appreciation for the lyrics and musicality is obvious, and that makes us feel we know him better. It builds trust and likability. Plus, there will be Dylan fans out there who *really* resonate with these posts and Dave builds a strong and loyal following this way.

Many social media experts will tell you to look up which national day it is or what's on trend to give you ideas about what to post. I'd urge caution in taking this approach. I was always taught by my Dad 'If you haven't got anything nice to say, don't say anything'. I think this can be adapted for an approach to posting on social media: 'If you haven't got anything interesting to say on a subject you really care about, don't say anything'.

Forcing your post to fit in with national 'blah blah blah' day is not interesting. Besides, these national days are becoming ridiculous! As I write this today it's National Avocado Day in the UK. Really?

Some people worry they'll only attract people who are into the things they're discussing, but I don't think that's true. Being honest always wins. Always. You know that about other aspects of your life. The same is true on social media and in your marketing materials. Speak from the heart with honesty and it will show.

Content Generator:

- What are you interested in outside of work?
- Can you relate your interests to the work you do?
- What can you teach us about the things you're interested in?
- Do you have a project on the go (training for a marathon, building a house)?
- Is there a weekly update you can give us about what you're doing?
- What does your hobby teach you about business or work?

SHOW WHAT YOU DO

Talking about what you do could seem like an obvious thing to do. However, it's often done in an advertising way. And as we know, this doesn't go down well. Putting up adverts is not adding value to anyone.

We need to take an approach that's informative and educational. As discussed earlier, what you do is fascinating to people who've never seen it before. You can take them through the process of what you do and explain each step.

For example, we have a client who supplies automatic packaging machinery, such as bottle or pouch fillers. The videos we've made for them have gone down really well. This is the type of process most people don't get to see regularly. Seeing these machines work, filling and capping bottle after bottle at speed can be quite compelling.

This is a great example of a process that can seem mundane to the people in the business. They might feel they have nothing interesting to show. But imagine a feed on their social channels showing these machines working, even simply, over and over every day. I could see a channel filled with simple footage, showing one part of the machine as the bottles/packets come through one section and the process repeats over and over. It's the kind of content that makes people stop scrolling and watch - there are probably channels devoted to this somewhere on the internet!

With a channel like that, you'd become known as *the* supplier of automated packaging machines. People will comment and share your posts and potential customers will begin to see them. The regularity with which you post, and the consistency of the content means people know what to expect. Without having to put up an 'advertising' type post, you've shown people what you do, added value to them (interest and entertainment) and established authority.

As we discussed earlier, repeating the same kind of content is absolutely fine - it's essential because not everyone in your network is going to see all your posts. You owe it to them to repeat your message, so they get to see your posts and benefit from the information you're posting.

Whatever your business, you have processes and methods for doing your work and a wealth of information. Share that, don't hold back - show people what you do, and demonstrate your knowledge and abilities. And do it in a way that adds value to your audience.

Content Generator:

- Think about everything you do - make a list
- Even if you think it's boring or obvious, write it down
- Break each process down and think about why you do it that way
- What can you explain about why you do things in a certain way?
- What do you do that people outside of your industry may have never seen?
- What do you do that your customers may be unaware of?

SHOW HOW YOU DO IT

Following on from showing what you do is the more controversial advice of showing *how* you do things. This is where people have the most resistance because they feel like they're giving away their industry knowledge and secrets to competitors and potential customers - who may do the thing themselves.

But the advice from the greatest content marketers out there is to give *everything* away. Of course, there will be processes you have to protect for legal or IP (Intellectual Property) reasons. I'm not suggesting you should show these. But be as generous as possible where you can.

By taking this approach, you're demonstrating your knowledge and generosity. Demonstrating your knowledge means you'll quickly be seen as the experts in your field. Being generous builds trust and people will want to work with you. Let's take an example from our industry, video production.

Lighting is key and will turn a video from average to exceptional. We could make videos every day and not explain it to anyone, almost treating it as an industry secret. Then when our videos come out, people can see they look exceptional but don't know why.

We have knowledge that others don't have, and we could see this as one of our secrets to beating our competition. However, suppose we share this knowledge on our social platforms. In that case, we're doing two things - we're demonstrating our knowledge and educating them on why our videos stand out from our competitors.

Sure, our competitors could copy our lighting techniques (and they have), but because we're the ones posting and educating people, we're seen as the experts when it comes to lighting and video. Our competitors may look up to us as well, which would have benefits down the line. They may have an enquiry they feel is outside of their abilities and pass that on to us. Potential employees will see we know what we're talking about and want to come and work for us - helping attract the best people.

The other concern people have is that by sharing this knowledge, your potential customers will just do it themselves. I'm here to tell you, once and for all - those people are *not* your potential customers! If they want to do it themselves, they will. That is simply the way they operate. And I say let them.

Not only let them but encourage and help them. You'll cement your position as the expert and when they move up to needing a higher level of product or service, who are they going to come to? You, of course. You've been generous with your knowledge and shown you know what you're talking about.

Most people will not do it themselves, and these people *are* your potential customers. To them, you're the expert in your field because you've been sharing all this great information and educating them. They're interested in what you do precisely because they're potential customers. The value of what you do is increasing in their eyes and it's becoming an easier purchase decision for them with every piece of information you share.

Think back to buying decisions you've made. What *type* of content did you consume before making that decision? How *much* content did you consume? You were probably deciding for a long time, especially for bigger purchases. How was that content delivered?

I expect, as you look back, the people you buy from are demonstrating their expertise through sharing knowledge and information regularly.

The hidden benefit of sharing how you do things is that it forces you to keep innovating and staying ahead of the curve. If you hold your industry secrets close and try to protect them, you may carry on doing things in the same way. While you're busy protecting your knowledge, your competitors are figuring out ways to innovate and overtake you.

However, if you're sharing how you do things, you need to innovate and keep moving forward to stay ahead. I realise this can be an unnerving concept, but I'm sure you wouldn't be reading this book unless you want to get ahead, innovate, and become an expert at what you do.

Content Generator:

- Think about how you do *everything*
- Can you explain the steps involved in each process?
- How and when did you learn to do it?
- What tips have you been given over the years?
- What are the small things you do which make a big difference?
- Why are your methods different/better?
- Have you given *everything* away? Honestly?
- Are you sure?

INSTRUCTIONAL

Providing instructions for how to use or service your product is a great piece of content for your website and social media. This can apply to service-based businesses too - see below.

I'm going to talk about providing an instructional video, but the advice here is equally applicable to a set of written instructions. Instructional videos can be easier for people to follow, and they provide you with a piece of content that can be used across different platforms.

The best approach is to create an instructional video and a set of written instructions to accompany it. That way, people can consume the information in whatever format suits them best - remember some people prefer the written word, while others prefer video or audio.

(Tip: once you've made your instructional video, get a transcript to help write the accompanying article)

An instructional video could take several forms. It could be showing how to assemble your product once the customer receives it. It could be taking them through the process of servicing the product, which needs to be done at regular intervals. Or it could be how to set up the product for optimum performance.

Instructional videos have several benefits to you as a business. Firstly, it's a great piece of generous, informative content which provides value to anyone considering buying your product. They can see how it goes together or how it's serviced and feel confident in their buying decision. They also build trust with you as a brand because they can see how well you look after your customers.

One thing that can really damage a brand's reputation is to leave your customers in the lurch after they've purchased from you. When purchasing one of the major appliances for our new house, I had a great call with the sales rep. He was super-enthusiastic on the phone, seemed like my best mate and was there to answer any questions I had.

After the sale had been agreed and I'd paid a deposit, I phoned up with a question. It was like he'd never heard of me, and I was being a pain by taking up his time. He'd moved on to chase the next sale. I felt like I'd been deceived, and all my brand loyalty disappeared. When people ask me for a recommendation, I tell them 'We used these people, they were ok, but I'm not sure I'd recommend them' - mainly because of the experience I had at this part of the buyer journey.

By producing an instructional video for your product, you're showing potential customers upfront that you care and will be there to support them. Of course, you must follow this up with great customer service and make sure you really *are* there for them!

Once your customer has bought your product, the instructional videos will be of great help. When they receive the product, they'll be able to watch the video to help them assemble it, and when it comes time to service the product, they'll do the same. All the time, you're building brand loyalty. Your customers will tell others how great you are and how easy you make it for them.

These videos also demonstrate the quality of your product. But crucially, you're doing it in a value-adding way. This is the opposite of 'advertising' where you're simply trying to push the product to people, telling them it's the best and they should buy. You're demonstrating how great it is, how helpful you are and building that all-important trust.

When you have an assembly or service video, you not only have a great marketing asset, you also have a means of cutting down on your customer service time too. If you currently receive calls and emails asking how things go together, how to service the product or how best to maintain it, an instructional video can answer all these questions.

By directing people to that video (or series of videos), you cut down on your customer services time answering calls. This could be a significant saving. We often tell our clients (who are usually in marketing) they should be asking for budget from customer services for these videos too, because they're going to see a huge benefit.

The more content you have out there about your product, the more easily people are going to find you. If you post these instructional videos on your website and YouTube, for example, it's going to help your SEO. Remember, YouTube is currently the second biggest search engine after Google. And being owned by Google, it only helps your SEO there too.

One of our clients recently told us about a sale through their YouTube channel because of the company video we made for them. This doesn't sound like a big deal if you have an active YouTube channel, but their channel was not particularly active at all. It's not a channel they'd been focusing on, so it was quite a surprise. You can imagine what might be possible if they built that channel with more quality, useful and value-adding content.

We've talked about physical products here, but the same approach can be used for services too. There's an instructional element to demonstrating your process for delivering your service. You can talk people through the process, so they know what to expect when they book with you. As with physical products, you'll build trust and demonstrate your expertise to potential customers, as well as cutting down on customer service time.

Content Generator:

- Is your product assembled by the customer?
- Does your product need regular servicing by the customer?
- What questions do you get regularly from customers about your product or service?
- How do you deliver your service once a customer buys from you?
- How will they receive their product?
- When will they receive their product?
- How do they go from receiving to using their new product?
- Do you already have an FAQ section you can turn into videos?

PRODUCT REVIEW VIDEO

Everybody loves a product review video - it helps us decide what to buy and provides some real-life feedback from someone who's not affiliated with the product or brand they're talking about. As a manufacturer, there are two types of product reviews you can make - one for the products you use in your business, and the other for the products you make and sell.

Firstly, a way to add value to your audience is to show and review the products you use in your business every day. I'm not necessarily suggesting you make in-depth product review videos - you can simply talk about the products you use, explaining why you chose them and how you find them. This is a form of behind-the-scenes video and provides an insight into what you do.

You're also delivering extra value to your audience by helping them decide on which products to choose. You can tag in the manufacturer of the product (unless it's a particularly bad review!) for some extra social media juice.

Remember, products include software - it doesn't have to be physical products only. For example, we've recently moved to a different video editing software. We can post about that experience, showing people what we use, why we use it and why we recommend it.

Secondly, for the products you make and sell yourself, you can ask other people to do product reviews. Affiliate marketing is a great way to get your product or service out to a larger audience. If you're not familiar with this, it involves finding people in your space who have a large following and would be willing to make a video talking about you. They'll share this video on their platform and their audience will get to see your product.

Sometimes these people are known as influencers because they have some influence in the genre they talk about. Some influencers will be happy to make a video in return for free product, and others will have a fee they charge for doing so. Either way, consider their audience and whether your product or service would be relevant to them.

Many influencers also make money with affiliate links. In this case, you'll give them a discount code or a custom link to post. When one of their viewers clicks the link or uses that discount code, they get a cut of the sale from you. In other words, you pay for each sale they generate. There are various tools out there to automate this process, so you can provide links and manage the influencers you have onboard.

One thing to mention; a lot of people know how this works with influencers getting free product or payment in return for posting about you on their platforms. This can make them sceptical about believing those people. Make sure that when you choose influencers, they're going to be honest and genuine. You don't want your brand to be associated with someone being inauthentic.

Content Generator:

- Which products do I use on a regular basis to do my work?
- Which products does everyone else in the business use?
- Why did we choose these products?
- What are the benefits to us personally of using these products?
- What are the benefits to the business?
- Would I recommend this product to others?
- Who are the influencers in your industry?
- Would they be willing to make a video about your product?

WHAT DO YOU TAKE FOR GRANTED?

There are probably things you take for granted every day. You do them without thinking, almost on autopilot, and don't consider them to be interesting. You may even assume everyone knows how that thing works or why you make those decisions.

You probably also know many people within your industry. They're used to seeing the same things you see every day, and it's 'normal'. You all use the same terminology and acronyms and have the same challenges. And you all know how everything works, you've been doing it for years!

However, these things are not obvious to other people outside of your industry.

For example, graphic designers who've been in the business for decades. When designing, they make decisions on things which are almost subconscious. The spacing between letters, the positioning of a title with respect to an illustration, the colour of the text, the type of font - the list goes on. They may not think others will be interested in these small decisions they make every day because it seems like second nature.

Put yourself in the shoes of someone outside your industry. Or indeed, put yourself back in your own shoes when you just started. Remember how it felt during your first week at the company. No doubt you were shown around and had things explained to you. You'd never seen how things were done before; it was all new. That is the person you're speaking to in your marketing content.

You probably had loads of questions about how things work. Why is the metal fed into the cutter this way, how is it held in place, and how long does it take to finish that process? After 6 months, these things all became normal to you - every day you come in, see the same process taking place or you use the same principles to design a brochure, product or part.

But remember, it's not normal to those outside your industry and by explaining things to us, you're creating fascinating content that adds value to our day by educating us.

If I come away from having a quick scroll on LinkedIn or YouTube having learnt how something works or how a decision is made, I feel quite fulfilled by that experience. I'll associate you and your brand with that feeling and build trust with you. I may even share the information I've seen with others.

Don't fall into the trap of thinking no one's interested in all these things - I promise you they are. You'll demonstrate your expertise and educate people at the same time. Focus on the latter, the former will happen as a result.

Think consciously about what you do each day. Make a note of how you do things, why you do things and what's involved. Keep it handy, in your pocket or on your desk. Those notes are now a list of content ideas for you.

If you're struggling with this, you could bring someone else in - an outsider with no experience in your industry - and show them around. Find out what interests them and the questions they have about what you do. In the mastermind group I run, we sometimes spend a session coming up with content ideas for each other. It can be a lot easier to generate ideas for other people because you're seeing what they do as unusual.

Content Generator:

- How did you make the decision to do something a certain way?
- Are there concepts or principles you followed to make that decision?
- What are the alternatives to doing it that way?
- What are the benefits of your way?
- Is there a written/documented process for what you're doing?
- What are your processes for doing those things?
- How were those processes developed?
- Which software do you use and why?
- What's your machinery of choice for a certain task?
- Where did you buy your machinery from?
- How long does it take to do this process?
- What have you learned about your profession over the years?

SHARING GOOD NEWS

Sharing good news goes down well on social media, I'm pleased to say. Remember your network is likely to be in your industry, or at least interested in your industry. They support that industry and want it to succeed. Therefore, good news stories will be well received. They'll cheer you on for sharing and thank you for promoting the industry in general.

There are people on social media who've created a whole brand around this idea. They put themselves forward as a champion of the industry by sharing good news stories. People resonate with it, and it makes them feel good - this is adding value to their day.

In the area we serve, manufacturing, there's often bad news in the mainstream media - as there is about everything. That's all they share and report on because they want to keep people scared so they'll keep watching their news channels. Your social media feed and email newsletter are a chance to counter this and show people there are plenty of good things going on in the world.

It can be easy to fall into the trap of sharing bad news because we see how effective it is at capturing people's attention. The classic marketing techniques tell you to scare people into thinking they're missing something or that they need your product, so they don't fall behind. These have worked for a reason - we're hardwired to be drawn towards bad news for survival. That's why the mainstream new channels are so effective.

But sharing good news on your channel is much better for your brand in the long run. Wouldn't you prefer to be associated with positivity and optimism, rather than negativity and scare tactics? Negativity can only go one way in my opinion - down. Positivity and optimism go upwards, lifting the people around you and bringing success for everyone.

You may need to actively get away from negative sources of news by limiting your intake. If you find yourself hearing negative news sources multiple times a day, it *will* bring you down and affect the content you're putting out there yourself. It might be a good idea to limit that influence in your life.

So, find good news within your industry and tell people about it. Share the optimism and counter the negativity we see so often. People will get behind you and support what you're doing.

To find these good news stories, there are industry-specific platforms reporting on the news in your sector, for example, Zenoot.com in manufacturing. I'd suggest subscribing to their email list for some great insights. You can also set up news alerts for certain keywords on Google, so when they're mentioned in news stories, you'll get an email.

Content Generator:

- Listen out for good news within your industry and make a note
- Set up news alerts on search engines for articles relating to your industry
- Subscribe to industry-specific platforms like Zenoot.com
- Investigate negative news stories and see if they're being truthful - can you counter this story with the real facts?
- Challenge yourself to post a positive news story at least once a week

PROMOTE OTHERS

Promoting others in your social posts or on your website is a fantastic way to provide value - both to the people you're promoting and to your audience, to whom you're recommending this person/company.

When you promote and recommend others, it's important to remember your reputation is on the line as well. You need to make sure you have full trust in the people you're recommending. They'll potentially be looking after one of your clients who will always have it in mind that you recommended them in the first place. If they perform poorly for any reason, it reflects badly on you.

But don't let that put you off. You know the good people in your network, and they will take on the responsibility of being referred, making sure they provide a great service to your clients and contacts.

When you make a post to promote someone else, it should be an entirely selfless act. Sing the praises of that person, talk about the incredible work they do and why you're recommending them. They'll no doubt be very flattered and may even share your post with their network. But again, to reiterate, don't make a post simply with the hope it'll be shared by them. It will be obvious and won't come across as genuine.

I like to combine my behind-the-scenes posts with recommendations. When the team sends me behind-the-scenes photos/videos to post on our company page, I'll talk about the work we're doing, but then also promote the client. It might be the product or service they provide. Or it might be how prepared and helpful they've been during the shoot.

Either way, my intention is to promote them, and my goal is to drive some business their way. Because this benefits everyone.

On occasion, I've posted some behind-the-scenes content while on a shoot, mentioned the great work the client does and had people contact them the very same day with an enquiry! Very satisfying.

Content Generator:

- Who would you genuinely recommend for products or services and why?
- Can you make a post while you're working for/with people to promote them?
- What specifically have they done that you'd recommend?
- This might be as simple as making you a great cup of tea, or it could be solving a complex manufacturing problem
- If you're making a testimonial video, be sure to talk about the great work your customer does too
- Your goal is to get that person some business - it will lift everyone - take the challenge!

ASK

When done properly, asking questions in your social posts can be an effective way to communicate and add value to your network. However, it needs to be authentic and genuine. We've all seen those posts asking questions simply to get engagement.

People like to be asked; there's something in our human nature that wants to give recommendations or advice. Asking a question can show some degree of vulnerability. You're not saying you know all the answers, you're genuinely asking for advice, a recommendation, or opinions on something.

Asking a question can also help position you as a leader in your space, if done correctly and coming from a genuine desire to help. By asking a question about something in your industry, you show that you're in touch and interested. You care about your colleagues and what's happening.

Of course, you'll get responses to your question and it's important to respond back. After all, people have taken the time to write a reply, so at least say thank you - even if you don't agree with their response. Engaging with comments on your post is important for the ol' algorithm - it likes to see that you're active and being social.

But regardless of what the algorithm thinks, you'll get more satisfaction and enjoyment from the conversations if you're actively engaging. If you're enjoying it, you're more likely to keep going *and* build a stronger network - which ultimately leads to more business.

Content Generator:

- What do you genuinely need help with at the moment?
- What's going on in your industry that you're genuinely interested in?
- Are you looking to buy a new product or service?
- Would you like some feedback on a new product or service you offer?
- Can you combine your question with some behind-the-scenes of your process?

WHAT ARE THEY ASKING YOU?

The questions you get asked regularly by your customers and/or prospective customers are gold dust.

Keep a note of them and when you're making content, simply pick the next one from the list. This content can either be quick social media videos or official company marketing assets for your website. Or both.

Sometimes I like to make the quick social media version of something, then later, turn that into a polished marketing video. It gives you a chance to practice the delivery, see what the response is (are there additional questions), and then perfect the final piece.

If you have a sales or customer service team, ask them to keep a note of questions they're asked regularly. As you compile a list, you'll see there are common threads. These are the topics you can address in your posts.

The polished videos you make answering these questions can be used on your website in an FAQ section. As we discussed earlier, posting these videos on your YouTube channel will give you an extra boost in your SEO too.

The fact people are asking you these questions in person probably means they're also searching for them online. Having *your* answers appear for people in search is what you want. If they have a question about a subject and see that you've answered it for them, you're now the expert in their eyes. There's a good chance they'll take the next step of finding out what you offer and may well purchase from you.

There are also various online tools available to find out what people are searching for; I like answerthepublic.com. You can input your subject and it gives you a list of all the search terms people are using around that topic. You can create content - blog posts, social posts, YouTube videos - using those exact search terms. The search engines will then match your post to those search terms and bring people to your content.

(Note: Of course, I've over-simplified this process and I'm not an SEO expert - it's a specialist subject with plenty of technicalities, but this is a good starting point for making content that people need.)

AI tools are also available now. At the time of writing, I haven't experimented with AI tools too much yet. I'm treating them with some degree of caution, simply on the basis that I don't want my content to be the same as everyone else's AI-suggested content. However, they're going to become an everyday tool which will help with generating ideas and my feeling is that if we enhance those with our own creativity, these new tools will help, rather than make us sound generic.

So, make sure you're always listening to your customers and potential customers, then use the tools available in the right way to find out what others are asking about your sector.

Content Generator:

- What are people emailing and phoning you about?
- What are they asking you at trade shows?
- What are your sales reps and retail outlets being asked?
- Make a list of these questions and then answer them in your marketing and sales content, either through blog posts or videos
- Create an FAQ section on your website with this content
- Use an online tool to discover what people are asking about

MAKING CONTENT IS CONTENT

Everything you do is an opportunity to create marketing content, as we discussed in the Behind-the-Scenes section. And that includes...the actual making of marketing content!

When you're creating a video, taking a picture for your socials, or having a video created by an agency, take the opportunity to make some content about that. Film and take photos behind the scenes of the filming taking place.

As we discussed earlier, people love to see behind the scenes of what goes on in your business - and that includes how you make your marketing content. I guess we all like to think we're getting an exclusive peek at what's happening. And even though it's going out on social media for anyone to see, it feels as though we're the only ones who get to see behind the curtains. We feel part of that process and it buys us into the brand even more.

For example, while writing this book, I've made several social media posts talking about the process, the challenges and what I've learned.

While you're making your content, show people what you're doing - explain the process, just like you would with any other process you show them. Talk about the challenges and why you chose to do things a certain way. Tag in the people helping you make the video or taking the pictures. As with anything, be generous.

Content Generator

- Take photos or film yourself as you're making content
- Show how it's being done
- Talk about the people helping you
- Show where you're filming or writing
- Explain why you're making this content
- Talk about the tools you're using to create and post your content

CONFIDENTIALITY

In some industries, there are confidentiality issues with sharing information about what you do. This could affect your ability to show a process or product. Or it could affect how much information you can divulge about a customer's success.

Examples of this could include manufacturers not being able to show a product being made because it's for a sensitive customer or pre-patent. Or accountants not being able to talk about their customer's increase in revenue.

In this case, think about ways to share what you're doing without divulging confidential information. We were discussing this on a recent mastermind call where an accountant faced the exact issue I described above. The advice from one of our members, Jon Johnson, was to look at the benefits to the client in a different way - in terms of their lifestyle, their ability to take holidays with the family and spend time with their children.

In the case of manufacturers not being able to show products, or premises that aren't looking at their best, think about the camera angles you're using and blurring out the background. Early in my photography career, I was photographing someone working on a submarine part which couldn't be shown. I zoomed right in on the part, only showing the hands of the person working on it.

Sometimes you can simply spin around and shoot in the other direction to make a facility look better. Or blur out the background using a shallow depth of field or portrait/cinematic mode on your phone.

You can also talk about the process, rather than discussing the specifics of the product being manufactured. Focus on the decisions being made, the tools being used and the benefits of both.

Sometimes the fact you can't show a product or divulge information is cut and dry. There's an NDA in place and everyone knows where they are. But if you don't have that agreement in place and you're just concerned about showcasing a customer's success or telling people you work with them, you might find it's not as much of a problem as you thought.

Ask them and find out. I know that can seem easier said than done, but you may be surprised to find they're very happy for you to talk about their case. Usually, if you've done a good job for them, they'll be happy to support you in any way they can.

We make a lot of testimonial/case study videos for our clients and one of the concerns they often have beforehand is whether their customers will be willing to give their time to appear on camera and talk about their experiences. Once they ask, it's very rare to be turned down.

People appreciate being asked to take part in something like that. You're saying 'We really value you as a customer' when you ask them to do this. And if they don't want to take part, they'll likely have a personal reason for not wanting to do it. They won't think badly of you for asking - they'll probably be apologetic for not wanting to.

Content Generator

- Can you demonstrate the benefits you bring in a different way?
- Can you show another aspect of the process that doesn't involve showing their product?
- Can you anonymise them enough when you write up or film a case study?
- Have you asked them or are you assuming they won't want to talk about the work you've done for them?
- How can you film/photograph your facility from a different angle that doesn't show the 'busy' or sensitive areas so much?
- Can you zoom in on a section of the product so it's not obvious what it is?
- Is there a break in production when you can come in and film without the sensitive products being on show?

LEGALITIES

Just to be clear, this section does not constitute legal advice!

If you're dealing with sensitive or confidential information, or giving advice on a subject, consider there may be some legalities involved in the way you can describe that or the claims you can make.

Facts and figures need to be checked in advance to make sure your claims are genuine. Hopefully, you're not operating this close to the limit of legalities, because it feels insincere to be making claims that need to be checked this closely.

But if you're working in a sensitive sector like financial advice, you may have to be careful not to make bold claims about investments or opportunities.

Every sector will have guidelines and you'll know where you have to exercise caution if you work in one of these areas. Your governing body (like the FCA – Financial Conduct Authority) will have guidelines and be able to offer specific advice.

As a general principle, we should be generous with our advice. If you find yourself having to alter words in case you're at risk of being sued, there's a chance you're trying to manipulate the data for your own gain. This is not a generous act and therefore not the type of marketing we're condoning in this book.

When in doubt, imagine yourself on the receiving end of the content you're making. Would you be genuinely grateful to receive the advice you're giving?

Content Generator

- Is what I'm telling people accurate?
- Can it be backed up with facts and if so, am I sharing those facts?
- Is my advice sincere or am I manipulating facts/statistics for my own gain?
- Are there any legal guidelines for presenting the information I'm sharing?
- Can my governing body help?
- Would I be genuinely grateful to receive the information I'm posting?

ASK OUTSIDERS

We've talked a lot about showing your processes; behind the scenes of what you do, how you do it and why. And I've prompted you to think about these things. However, I realise it can still be difficult to see things from another perspective.

If you need more input, I suggest asking outsiders for their ideas and questions.

When we go into businesses to make marketing videos, a lot of the time people will tell us "We don't really have much here, it's a bit boring". But coming in with a fresh pair of eyes, we *always* find it interesting to see what goes on - how things are done and why. From that perspective, it's much easier to generate ideas for marketing content.

Find someone outside your business who you trust - preferably someone naturally interested and inquisitive. Ask them what they'd like to know about what you do. Show them around your facility and make a note of all their questions.

Content Generator:

- Who can you ask who's naturally inquisitive and unfamiliar with your industry?
- Show them around, explain what you do and make a note of their questions
- Use these questions to create marketing materials; written or video
- Which things seemed obvious to you, but not to them?

EXAMPLES

In this section, I'm giving some examples of the type of content different businesses could make. I'm starting with a manufacturing business, and then demonstrating the same for accountants and graphic designers, to show how the principles can be applied to any business. I like to look outside of my own industry for inspiration because often, the way people do things in their industry can be directly transferred to ours.

Example: Product Manufacturing

I've seen countless examples of people in manufacturing thinking they've got nothing of interest to show in their marketing materials. This couldn't be further from the truth and was the inspiration for this book. Manufacturers have a lot going on, but to them, it can appear normal.

Here are some ideas for product manufacturers:

- How does the design process work?
- What software do you use to design your products?
- What considerations need to be made at the design stage?
- How does a small change in design affect production?
- What tolerances do you work to and why?
- What tolerances are achievable in production?
- How do you communicate the design to production?
- Who's involved in the design and sign-off process?
- How do you set up a milling machine (or any other machine) ready to start production?

- How do you sharpen the tools?
- Which machines or tools do you prefer and why?
- Meet the people with the skills, interview them
- Where do you source raw materials from?
- What qualities do you look for in raw materials?
- How are raw materials delivered?
- How do the machines or tools work?
- What is their capability and capacity?
- How many products do you make each day/week/month/year?
- How long does it take to train as a machinist?
- What are the career opportunities?
- What do you enjoy about your work?
- What was your journey or career path to this point?
- How is the product assembled?
- How do you package the product for shipping?
- Who do you sell to?
- Where do you sell to?
- How big is the business and/or premises?

Example: Accountants

On the face of it, accountancy seems like it could be difficult to generate content ideas for. But I've seen accountants who post a *ton* of content every day. A friend, Sharon Baker, is fantastic at this - in fact, it was a generous post about the benefits of buying/leasing a car that put us in contact in the first place.

Here are some ideas for accountants:

- What is VAT and how does it work?
- How to use accounting software

- Shortcuts, tips and techniques for using accounting software
- What is a Profit and Loss report?
- Why you would need a P&L report
- What happens at my year end?
- When do I need to pay tax?
- Tax law changes and how they affect you
- Should you buy or lease a car?
- Employment laws and PAYE tax
- How to be more tax efficient as a business owner
- Meet the team, behind the scenes in the office
- How you got into accountancy
- Why you love accountancy
- Promoting your clients (with their consent)
- Client success stories (again, with their consent)
- The process of completing a tax return
- What's a personal tax return?
- How you can use accounting software to be more efficient
- Invoicing tips and tricks
- How to get paid faster
- When to use finance in your business
- How to manage your bank account and save for the things you need, like tax, insurance etc.
- Which banks do you recommend?
- Which software do you recommend?
- How do you onboard new clients?
- Transferring from your old accountant, how it works
- How our fee structure works

Example: Graphic Designer

I know some graphic designers don't think that what they do is interesting. I'm always amazed at what goes into the process when I discuss it with friends like Ian Woodley and Jane Anson.

As with any business, they've got used to it over the years and forgotten just how interesting it is to those who don't understand it.

Here are some ideas for graphic designers:

- How to lay out a flyer, poster, web page, bottle label etc.
- What considerations do you make when laying out anything for the first time?
- What information do you need from your client to begin designing?
- How do you choose a font (this can be repeated every time you design something new)?
- Font spacing - why it matters and how to decide
- Vertical line spacing - how to decide on this
- What are the different file types your client will receive?
- What's the difference between the file types?
- What are the benefits of each file type?
- Which software do you use and why?
- How did you get into graphic design?
- What does your day look like?
- How do you come up with creative ideas (go for a walk, meditate, have a shower, sit at your desk, brainstorm etc.)?

- What's your favourite pencil/pen for sketching and why?
- Are there sketching apps you use or recommend?
- What's the difference between CMYK and RGB?
- What's Adobe RGB?
- What does resolution mean and why is it important?
- What's a pixel and how does it relate to DPI when printing?
- How do you choose colours?
- Are there relationships between colours I should consider?
- Do some colours signify different things (e.g. red for danger)?
- What are brand guidelines and why do they matter?

CHAPTER SUMMARY

You now have some practical ways to generate ideas for your social media marketing content. You have huge potential sitting right in front of you, and just by looking at it differently you can create GREAT content following these principles.

If you haven't already, I encourage you to take some time to do an initial brain dump of ideas. Go back and follow the content generator bullet points at the end of each section. Starting is the key and then ideas will flow. View your business from a fresh perspective and you'll realise that everything you do and know is interesting to others.

Now we're going to move on to discuss some practicalities when it comes to making your own social media videos.

CHAPTER 7
SOCIAL MEDIA VIDEOS - PRACTICALITIES AND TIPS

GETTING SOCIAL

When it comes to social media, the simple advice I like the most is 'get social'. This tells you all you need when it comes to tactics and strategy. Getting social means treating these platforms as if you were in a real-life, in-person social setting.

When you walk into a room full of people, you don't just spurt out a line of advertising. You start talking to people, listening and contributing to the conversation. Furthermore, when you say something, the person you're talking to responds, you respond back and so on. I know this sounds simple - how to have a conversation - but too many people still treat social media like an advertising billboard when it comes to business.

For personal use, they'll use it to have conversations, but when it comes to business, they feel the need to post some form of 1960s advert! Which of course, no one replies to because that's not what they're there for.

Imagine yourself going into that virtual room to have conversations and meet people. See what value you can bring to the room. Respond to comments and questions people leave on your posts. People will engage with you this way and you'll also enjoy the process more - it's a win-win.

HOW TO SHOOT VIDEO FOR SOCIAL

When making your own social media videos, there are a few things you can do to enhance the quality, without needing to hire a production company.

Sound and lighting are key. The quality of the audio is critical to making a decent video. Some people say it's more important than the footage. It's true you can get away with a poor-quality video if you have decent audio. But regardless of how amazing the footage is, if the audio quality is poor, the video will feel unwatchable and turn people away.

Let's assume you're filming with your phone. To ensure you have good-quality audio, make sure you're in a quiet location with no (or limited) background noise. You don't want anyone to start speaking in the background or have noisy machines nearby. The quality of the microphone on most modern phones is decent. I've made plenty of videos of myself taking to camera using my phone's inbuilt microphone and as long as there's no background noise, it's perfectly acceptable.

To move up to the next level, you can use your headphones as the microphone - earbuds or wired headphones. To make it sound pro, you can attach an external microphone to your phone. There are various types available, but I'd suggest a Lavalier microphone - the small ones that clip onto your collar. You may need to use an interface; this is a small device that plugs into your phone and then allows you to plug in a microphone.

Lighting is also critical. We've all been on a video call with someone who has a window directly behind them. It's super bright and the camera is trying to balance out the brightness by making everything darker - including their face. As a result, their face is completely dark, and we can't make out what they look like. Not great for that all-important trust factor!

Aim to have your face evenly lit. A simple way to achieve this is by positioning yourself just in front of a window, but where you're not in direct sunlight. A north-facing window is ideal, but any window will do, as long as the sun isn't shining directly onto your face. The reason for this is that the sun produces very hard shadows on your face.

If you go out into the midday sun, for example, take a photo of yourself and observe the light and shadows on your face. You'll see there are hard shadows, which may be causing your eyes to look very dark - we call it panda eyes. Now if you walk into the shade, you'll see the light evens out over your face. It's a lot more gentle and pleasing.

If you don't have a window or it's not convenient to be near one, look at getting some artificial lighting for your desk or wherever you plan to set up your camera. There are various ones available, the LED panels and ring lights are effective and will give you a nice even light. You want a relatively large light source, so the light spreads out evenly over your face.

Next, think about the background we can see in your video - what's behind you. Ideally, you want a nice clear and clean background. A messy office or dirty area of the factory won't give the best impression. Consider using the cinematic mode on your phone's camera which will artificially blur the background for you. This helps bring the focus back to your face and hides messy areas.

Finally, you need to be aware of your framing and how you hold the camera. By framing, we mean the position of yourself within the picture. Are you right at the bottom of the frame, or is your head going off the frame at the top or sides? Aim to have yourself positioned in the centre of the frame and don't be too close to the camera - give us some space!

Make sure you're holding the camera straight and level when recording. Again, we've all seen people on calls and social media videos where their camera is really low, and we can see straight up their nose! It's not a great look.

Using a tripod or some kind of stand for your phone makes the video look that much more professional. You can buy a simple phone holder clip and a small tripod or desk-mounted stand (or you can make one using a wine bottle and elastic band!).

If you're holding your phone by hand, make sure you hold it steady and level. I'd always suggest using the front-facing camera when filming yourself so you can see how the framing is looking as you record. Don't move around too much, or we'll get dizzy watching you.

Ideally, if you're going to be moving around, use a gimbal to hold your phone. This is a device that will keep the phone straight and level as you move, removing most of the unwanted movements you make with your arm. They stabilise the phone so your footage looks smooth and far more professional.

When filming or photographing the facility, think about the angles you're filming from. A row of identical machines or workbenches viewed from a certain angle can look very satisfying for example. Try getting down very low or getting up very high for a different perspective. Take your time to 'look' properly – you may be amazed at how different things look when you stop and sit somewhere you wouldn't normally sit. Again, it's about viewing your facility from a different perspective and seeing it with fresh eyes.

In summary, the things you need to consider when making social media videos using your phone are:

- Audio quality - background noise and microphone quality
- Lighting - ensure your face is evenly lit without harsh shadows or panda eyes
- Background - what's behind you, does it look professional?
- Framing - make sure you're in the centre of the frame
- Tripod or stand - keep the phone steady on a stand or hold it still
- Camera angle - ensure the camera is straight and level, not low and pointing up at you
- Experiment with different angles when filming the facility.

TALK TO ONE PERSON

When you begin making videos of yourself talking to camera, it can be daunting. I certainly found it that way the first few times I did it! You can feel silly talking to yourself, even if you know no one's watching. And you worry about what all those *thousands* (if not millions) of people are going to think of you when you post it!

Well, fear not. Firstly, it's unlikely that many people are going to see your video - at least to begin with when you have a small following. Secondly, it will be a lot better than you think. You'll come across well - after all, you're giving this a shot, you're out there doing it and people will respect that. You know what you're talking about - you're an expert in your field, so have confidence in your abilities.

A great tip for not worrying about all those people watching you is to imagine yourself simply talking to one person when you hit record. You probably already have an ideal customer profile. Hopefully, you've got specific with that, you've given them a name, and know a little about them and their home life, hobbies, business etc. Getting granular with this will help with your confidence when speaking on camera.

Now when you hit record, imagine yourself talking to that person, and that person only. That is who you're making this video for, and it doesn't matter what anyone else thinks. It's almost like you're making a personal video message for them.

If you're like 99% of the population, you'll also be prone to pausing and filling the gap with 'umm' when thinking about your next words. The best tip I have for this is to simply pause when you feel an 'umm' coming on. The pause may feel like an eternity, but I promise you, it will feel like nothing to those watching. Slow down and take your time.

It might take a few attempts to get it right and this is normal. Start and see how you get on. If you mess up, there's no pressure - just delete and try again. Remember that starting is the hardest part!

EDITING AND APPS

Once you've recorded your video, it may need a little trimming and polishing. This can be done very easily using the standard camera app on your phone, or you might choose to use a third-party video editing app. Trim out the beginning and end where you're getting ready to speak. You need to go straight in with a compelling first line - a hook. People have a lot of content to choose from in their feeds, so let's get going straight away.

You can simply trim the beginning and end of the video by dragging the start and end points along.

Now, if you want, you can add captions to your video - the ones that pop up as you speak, or simply appear gently on the screen below. Some of the social platforms, like LinkedIn, will add these for you automatically - although I'd always check they've got it right and edit them if necessary. There are also third-party apps out there for adding captions. I'm not going to list them here, because it's a fast-changing world and I'll be out of date before I hit publish!

Have a look around and try some out. You'll see there are other tools available too, like AI noise removal (just check the final audio doesn't sound like you're underwater - and always try to get it as good as possible in-camera first) and AI social shorts generators. When I started writing this book, these were not performing all that well, but they've already improved a lot.

If you do nothing else, just tidy up your video before posting so we don't see the awkward parts before and after you speak.

UPLOAD VIDEO

When you come to upload your video onto your chosen social platform, remember to upload directly to the platform, rather than posting a link to YouTube. Of course, YouTube might be your chosen platform and perhaps you're trying to drive people towards YouTube from your other social media. But as a general rule, upload directly to the platform you're posting to.

The reason is that each platform wants people to stay there. Let's take LinkedIn as an example. They want users to stay on LinkedIn, so if you post a link to your video over on YouTube, that post is going to be downgraded by 'the algorithm' - essentially meaning it won't be shown to as many people.

The same goes for *any* external links on these platforms - if you include a link to your website in your posts, they'll also be downgraded. Instead, tell people to go to your profile, where they'll be able to find your web link.

TAGGING PEOPLE

Tagging people in your post is a good way to increase the reach of that post. Currently on LinkedIn, if you tag someone into your post, their followers (or at least some of them), will see they've been tagged - your post will be shown to a wider audience.

Be careful not to get spammy with it. Only tag people into posts in a genuine, authentic and helpful way. A great way to do this is to give people a shout-out or say thank you. Again, make sure it's genuine.

The algorithm also notices when the people you've tagged respond to your posts. So, if you tag me and I 'like' or comment on that post, it tells the algorithm it was a genuine tag - not just done to increase your reach. And if it thinks it's genuine, it will show the post to more people.

HASHTAGS

I like to compare hashtags with dividers in ring binders. With ring binders, we used to include dividers so you could easily find the section you wanted. They stick out a little from the paper in the binder so you can put your finger on them and go directly to that section.

Hashtags are similar, in that people can search for posts on a particular subject by searching for that hashtag. Not only can you search for them, but you can also follow a hashtag in the same way you would follow a person.

It's good to include a few hashtags in your posts. It tells people what you're posting about, and your content will come up when they search for that subject or follow the hashtag. Your posts will be seen by more people and critically, more relevant people. For example, if you want to reach people in the automotive industry, use the hashtag #automotive or #automotiveengineering. The chances are your ideal clients will be looking at posts with that hashtag because they're interested in the automotive sector.

I like to include hashtags at the bottom of the post on a separate line. Some people include them in the body of the text, for example, "I was at a #factory yesterday when I noticed their #5axismillingmachine".

I find this more difficult to read and it feels as though the post is just there for reach/advertising. Ultimately, if your post is genuinely adding value and helping people, it doesn't matter where your hashtags go, I'm sure!

RESPONDING TO COMMENTS

Just as you would in a room full of people, it's important to respond to the comments you get on social media.

Not only do the algorithms like this - they see that you're active and not just posting and forgetting about it - but it also makes the process more enjoyable for you.

Social media platforms like to see that you're engaged with your audience and will reward this by showing your post to more people. They have one main objective - to keep people on their platform. If you're posting decent content and they can see that you're engaging with your audience, it will keep people on their platform.

For you, seeing comments and responding to them makes the whole process more enjoyable. You're meeting people, getting feedback, and understanding what your connections like. This is valuable information.

Of course, having real-life conversations trumps this every time! I'm not advocating hiding away in your office behind your computer all day, only having virtual conversations on social media. I'd much rather be out there meeting people in real life, any day. But as part of the marketing and business development mix, social media is a useful tool which can be more enjoyable if you decide to make it so.

One word of warning on responding to posts; remember this means writing decent responses to people who've commented on your posts. At the very least, 'thank you' or 'I really appreciate your comment'. A thumbs-up or smiling emoji (whilst it has its place!) doesn't count as a decent response.

I advise writing a response of at least 4 words (not including their name) to every comment you receive. Of course, there will be comments from people touting for work or advertising their own services on your posts. These generally don't warrant a response in my opinion, so just ignore them (or even delete them if you like).

CALL TO ACTION

A call to action is where you ask people to do something at the end of your post. This applies to social media posts, blog posts, email newsletters, etc. You'll need to have a clear idea of your goals to begin with - Target, from the GREAT approach.

In my opinion, you do need to be a little careful with your calls to action, especially on social media posts. You need to ensure you're adding value, always following the principles of GREAT. If you're not careful, adding a call to action in the wrong way can make that post seem less well-meaning than you intended.

I'd advise being gentle with your calls to action and giving people a good reason to take action. For example, if you're providing tips and advice, you could ask them to follow you or your own hashtag for more of the same. Or you could ask them to follow your company page. As discussed, social media platforms don't like external links, so as soon as you include a link to your website or to book a call, that post will be downgraded and won't be shown to as many people.

Some people have a standard footer on their posts which says who they are, what they do and how you can follow them for more. I really like this approach when it's done well. My friend Dave Rogers does this well and LinkedIn expert Ashley Leeds always includes a call to action to follow his hashtag.

Having people follow you, your hashtag or your business page is the first step to bringing them on board as a customer. From there, they'll see your content regularly, become familiar with you and what you do, and build trust.

In the long run, I'd encourage you to point people towards your email list, asking them to join to hear more from you. This is because, unlike the social media platforms, you own this asset. If for some reason you get kicked off social media one day, your account gets hacked or the platform goes down, you will still have your email list and therefore the ability to communicate with your audience.

CHAPTER SUMMARY

- Get social on social media – treat it as you would a room full of people.
- Join in conversations, ask questions, get to know people – connect.
- Sound quality is super-important when making your own videos.
- Try to eliminate background noise while filming.
- Use an external microphone for best audio quality.
- Lighting is critical too.
- Ensure your face is evenly lit with no harsh shadows.
- Film in front of a window without direct sunlight, or use a video light.
- Consider the background – does it look cluttered or messy?
- Use cinematic mode on your phone to blur the background.
- Framing is important – ensure you're positioned well within the picture and the phone is straight and level.
- Use a tripod for stationary shots, or a gimbal if you're moving around.
- View your facility from different angles to find interesting perspectives to film from.
- Sit for a while in areas you wouldn't normally sit and observe things from a new perspective.
- Imagine you're talking to one person when filming.
- At minimum, do a basic edit on your videos to trim the beginning and end, so you get straight into your message and captivate people right from the start.

- Upload your video directly to the social platform you're posting to (unless you're trying to build a YouTube channel, in which case you may want to direct people to a YouTube link)
- Tag people in your posts as long as it's genuine and authentic.
- Use hashtags to tell people what the post is about and enable them to find your posts more easily.
- Reply to comments with at least 4 words, in a helpful, authentic way.
- Include a gentle Call to Action

CHAPTER 8
CORNERSTONE VIDEO MARKETING ASSETS

S o far we've talked a lot about 'content' in this book and much of that focus has been on social media marketing videos.

In this section, we're going to look at the high-production value video marketing assets you can (and should) make. These are your cornerstone video content; the videos you show on your website and pin to the top of your social media channels. They're extremely valuable to your business, as you're defining your brand and communicating your company values within these videos.

A marketing asset like this can be used for several years, both in its produced form and as snippets for social content. The messaging needs to be right, in terms of what's said and how your business is portrayed visually. This requires discussion, advice, and planning, which is where a video production company and/or marketing agency comes in.

I like to see these videos as tools within your digital toolbox. As you would pull out a screwdriver to do up a screw, you can pull out your marketing videos to help achieve your marketing and sales goals.

One of the questions we get asked is 'What type of video could I create?'. Sometimes people have an idea for the type of video they'd like but maybe aren't aware of the other options. Occasionally we end up with a totally different type of video, one that fits their marketing objectives and use case better.

This section is relatively brief - it's a non-exhaustive list, meant as a prompt to show the types of videos you could make and get you thinking about what's possible with video.

The GREAT approach still applies to these cornerstone pieces of content. They can't be old-fashioned adverts. Let's have a brief look at how each part of the acronym might apply, to see how it differs from that of a social media marketing video:

GIVE. While you might not always be giving information or advice in these videos, remember that giving comes in different forms. It might be because the video is so pleasing to watch, you're giving people a great viewing experience. You may include special effects or humour to bring your video to life. Giving an insight into your business and the way you work is also a form of giving, helping people see what you're all about as they come through the buyer journey.

RECORD. You may be documenting a process you've been through, such as research and development, recording what you've done to help demonstrate your expertise and give people an insight into how you've developed a product. Letting people see behind the scenes can be done effectively in a company brand video. You may choose to shoot your video in a documentary style, so the viewer feels part of the process and learns more about you as a business.

EDUCATE. You should always be looking to educate your audience as part of the buyer journey. By educating them, you're helping them to understand why they might need you, the value you bring and why they can trust you. You can also produce educational videos such as assembly or service videos to help your customers, which we'll discuss below.

ADD VALUE. Adding value comes in many different forms. Remember to reward your viewers for investing time in watching your video. You need to add value to their day in some way. This could be through teaching them something, showing them something or entertaining them in some way. For example, your company or brand video is not just an advert about how great you are; it's a mini-documentary with some inspirational stories. The value you're adding in this case is to inspire people. At the same time, they're learning about your company. Leaving them feeling inspired is much more powerful than simply having told them how great you think you are.

TARGET. It's always important to know how and where your video will be used. With a cornerstone piece of video content, your audience could be different to that of your social media pieces. Depending on where they are along the buyer journey, a longer video may be appropriate because they're already interested in your company. If they're watching your video to help decide whether to invest a significant amount of money with you, they'll be happy to invest longer in watching and finding out about your company. However, if the investment is small (let's say you sell low-price widgets on Amazon), then a short, punchy product video is more appropriate. There are other factors to consider when it comes to your target audience and designing your cornerstone video content around this is critical. We'll look at this in more detail in the next chapter, before discussing the types of videos we can make.

When a customer sees that you've invested in a high-end video for your business, it gives them confidence that you do things properly in all areas. It's a bit like having a clean and tidy factory - when someone comes to visit and sees you look after things properly, it gives them confidence that you work to a high standard across the board. Having professional videos demonstrates your commitment to quality. This chapter will give you inspiration for where to get started, or how to carry on with your video marketing effectively.

HOW WILL YOU USE IT?

Sometimes, people have an idea for a video in their business but haven't thought about how they'll use it. A video sitting on your hard drive or posted once to social media could be worth absolutely nothing to you - and definitely not the thousands of £'s you invested in making it.

That's why the first question I always ask when people enquire about making a video is: How Will It Be Used?

Videos can be used in many ways throughout your marketing, sales and after-sales care process. They may be seen by an audience who *want* to see them (because they've intentionally searched for it on your website), or they may be on social media in amongst the ocean of content where the video needs to 'pop' and capture people's attention straight away. In these examples, the video should be designed and produced slightly differently.

Think about where your video will be used along the buyer journey. Is this purely a brand awareness video to help build an impression of your brand? Will it be used to invite your audience into a marketing funnel - in which case it needs to have a specific call to action? Or perhaps it's designed to help your customers once they've purchased from you.

During the sales process, you can use videos to help people along. You could send out a video explaining the next steps in your process, or if you have an in-person sales process, you might show a brand video while you're calculating a price, helping demonstrate your quality and service levels.

Once they're on board, you can use a video to thank them or hand over to your delivery team. An individual homemade video for that customer (on Loom or Vidyard for example) is a nice way to introduce a colleague on your team who'll be providing the service after they've been dealing with a sales rep.

Video length is always a critical question! We have a few standard-ish lengths we tend to go to for different types of video. Again, it depends where the video is going to be used. As we all know, there's a ton of content on social media and no one has much time to sit and watch. As a result, these videos tend to be quite short and snappy. There are also video length restrictions on certain platforms to be aware of. Knowing where your video will be posted is crucial in that respect.

Regardless of the length, on social media, it's good to have a captivating introduction (a hook) to pull people in and make them want to watch more. This should be followed by engaging content that keeps them watching.

If your video is high quality, people will want to watch it. I've been of the opinion for some time that having a longer video could help to self-select serious buyers. If someone is willing to watch a 10-minute video (a mini-documentary) about your business, there's a very good chance they'll become a loyal customer. Perhaps it's better to use this as a filter right at the start, rather than going through a less engaged audience and having to convince them with multiple videos.

I haven't tested this theory very rigorously yet, but I do know that a mini-documentary we made for a local civic society about a blacksmith's yard is one of our most watched videos on YouTube, running at 8 minutes in length. A slightly different thing of course because people are watching it out of interest. But why couldn't they be watching a mini-documentary about your business? I noted recently that Apple was showing an 8-minute advert for their new VR goggles on YouTube.

If your video will be used in a Pay-per-click (PPC) campaign, then you need to have a very specific call to action. You will have planned out your campaign and already know what you want your audience to do after they've watched the video - a free download, book a call etc.

Once you've invested in a stunning brand video as a marketing asset, the main thing is to get on and use it! Use it well and use it everywhere it makes sense. Make sure you go into the production process with a clear idea of your objectives so you can work with your video production agency to design the video and messaging in the right way.

BRAND VIDEO

The Brand Video (sometimes called a Company or Vision Video) is an overview of your company and/or brand. It's the video you show on the homepage of your website when people want to find out more about your business, the founders and the people who work there.

It may talk about your values, what you do, where you've come from and the outcomes you achieve for your customers. It can take the form of an interview with the founders, a professional presenter talking to your audience, a voiceover or text graphics. All of which can be used to get your message across and show who you are and what your brand is all about.

It's an opportunity to showcase your people. You could include interviews with employees, demonstrating their experience and passion for the industry.

The overall feel of the video should be in line with your brand. Are you an exciting, fast-paced, punchy brand, or do you need to be slower and more considered? The colours you use throughout the video will be important and should be on-brand, as well as the messaging.

As discussed earlier, adding value to your audience in your brand video could be through the stories you share, inspiring your audience and bringing them on board with your enthusiasm. You might show some behind-the-scenes, which again helps people buy into your brand, demonstrates your expertise, and adds value by giving some insight into what you do.

From a brand video, you can create a series of social media videos using snippets from the video itself, or other pieces of footage you shoot during the production process. These can be posted on your social media to tease in the main brand video, making people want to watch the whole thing when you release it.

Remember you could also shoot some behind-the-scenes footage on the day(s) of production. Use these on social media to create some buzz around the video before it comes out (and of course add value to people with behind-the-scenes insights).

Your Brand Video is an important piece of cornerstone content which should stay relevant for several years, ensuring you see a return on your investment many times over.

PRODUCT VIDEO

The Product Video is a showcase of one of your products. You demonstrate the features and benefits of the product, as well as the outcomes it will help achieve for your customer. You may show some use cases, or it may be a studio-based video where the product appears to float in space - think iPhone videos as an example.

If you have a service-based business, you can replace 'product' with 'service' throughout this section. Your video will focus on the service (or one of the services) you offer, showing the viewer what to expect and what outcomes you will bring for them.

You may have a presenter talking about the benefits of the product, a voiceover, or text graphics to communicate the key points.

Product videos can be used at different stages and for different reasons within your business. At product launch, for example, you'll be unveiling your product to the world (hopefully after talking about it for some time beforehand, so they're excited to hear about it). At this stage, a product video can take a certain style and you might make the most of the 'unveiling' part. Lights coming on gradually, for example, revealing the product from the darkness.

If your product is sold by a third party in a bricks-and-mortar store, they often have product videos showing at the counter. This will be a snappy, attention-grabbing video, showcasing your product to their customers while they wait.

Your product videos will of course sit on the product pages of your website. You can pin them to the top of your social media pages, and they can form the cornerstone of your content around that product.

The value you're adding to your audience here is to inform them of what they can expect from your product. You're helping them decide which product to select, demonstrating why yours is the best, and entertaining them in some way too.

Take the example of a counter video at a bricks-and-mortar store. If your video can entertain people while they wait, you've added something to their day and made an impression on them. They'll likely remember your brand, maybe even telling others about it and the impressive video they've just seen. At some point - maybe today, maybe next week, or maybe next year - they'll become a customer.

Product videos are one of our favourite types of videos to make. It's an opportunity to get creative with what could be a fairly mundane object. How do we show off the features? What angles can we show it from for the highest impact? How can we surprise our audience with shots they weren't expecting? And how can we light the product to make it look incredible?

Your product video is the culmination of all that hard work you've put into designing and producing it in the first place. It should make your product look amazing, providing foundational content you can refer to and use throughout your marketing.

TESTIMONIAL VIDEO

Testimonial Videos are interviews with one of your happy customers talking about the outcomes and transformation you've helped them achieve and recommending you to others. This is a powerful message because it's not coming from you, it's coming from a real-life customer; someone who's experienced working with you or using your product.

Apart from the kind words they're speaking about you, the fact they've taken time out of their busy schedule to do this for you speaks volumes. They clearly value the work you've done for them.

The proper marketing word for this is 'social proof'. Your website should be littered with social proof, whether through video or small snippets of reviews from happy customers.

As with all your videos, you can also create small teaser-style snippets for your testimonial videos - excerpts of just a line or two which you can use on social media. Your product or service will have solved a specific problem for your customer, so each testimonial video can focus on the outcome you've helped them achieve. Once you have a collection of testimonial videos, you'll be able to demonstrate how you've helped solve a variety of problems for your customers. These can be used by your sales team to show prospective customers who face the same issues.

Testimonial videos are a fantastic tool in your marketing mix. If you're just starting with video content, this is where I'd advise you to begin. Compared with some of the other videos listed in this section, they can be relatively straightforward to make. Sometimes people are hesitant to ask their customers for a testimonial, but in our experience, it's very rare for anyone to outright refuse - they're usually delighted to have been asked and more than happy to help.

CASE STUDY VIDEO

A case study video is similar to a testimonial video. However, we go into much more depth about their particular case; how you've helped them solve their problems and delivered your product or service to their sector.

Case study videos are used by your sales and marketing teams to demonstrate to potential customers how you've helped solve similar problems for similar customers. As with testimonial videos, they can be dispatched at various points along the buyer journey to provide your prospects with the confidence they need to become customers.

For larger organisations, you may have a series of case study videos covering a range of services and sectors. For example, if you can provide services to both the automotive and aerospace industries, you'd have a case study for each of these use cases.

It's also useful to accompany these with a written case study by a professional copywriter. As discussed earlier in the book, some people prefer to consume content in different formats and the words on your website will help boost your SEO.

To reiterate, asking your customers to help with a testimonial or case study video can seem daunting, but in my experience, the vast majority of people are more than willing to help. They've benefitted from your service or product and would like to see you succeed - remember it's in their interests too, because they'd no doubt like to buy from you again someday.

HOMEPAGE VIDEO

These are the videos that play automatically when you land on someone's website. They're typically shown full-bleed (i.e. the video extends to the edge of the page without a border) and without sound.

Apart from being more immersive and captivating than a still image, they also serve a purpose when it comes to your SEO. If you have a compelling video on your homepage, people will spend more time there when they land on it. This tells the search engines they've sent that person to a useful page and increases your page ranking.

Therefore, it's important the homepage video tells a story and takes people on a journey. I see many homepage videos that are simply a series of clips stuck together. They look nice, but they don't provide a reason for the viewer to stay. We're aiming for people wanting to find out what's going to happen next and stay longer.

The homepage video should demonstrate all areas of your business - the service or products you provide and the people delivering them. You may also incorporate text graphics to promote what you do or ask questions of the viewer. Sometimes these text graphics are overlaid on the website itself, but they can also be baked into the video with motion added for more impact.

Remember, when you have a homepage video, this will usually need to be hosted on your website itself - rather than embedding a YouTube or Vimeo link, as you would with your other videos. As such, it needs to be compressed efficiently so you don't lose quality, whilst making the file small enough to load quickly.

The homepage video is likely to be the very first impression people get of your business, so it needs to have impact, be on-brand and take the viewer on a journey to discover your capabilities.

INJECTING HUMOUR

Video with some humour can be a great way to show your brand in a slightly different light and grab people's attention in a busy online world. It's a difficult line to tread as the humour needs to be done with just the right tone.

Subtlety, along with clever scriptwriting, filming and editing are key. Keep it classy and you'll hit the right spot with this, creating a video that people want to show their friends and colleagues.

Of course, the humour must be appropriate for your brand and perhaps used in the right area. You may be able to use a bit of humour to promote one part of your service, rather than the main product offering. For example, we created a funny video for our client's Buyback offering, while their main product and promotional videos are more serious.

Even when making a serious video, however, the fun part is making them look epic – using dramatic lighting, special effects, music, and scripting to have a big impact.

RECRUITMENT VIDEO

The Recruitment Video is an underused asset. When recruiting, you're marketing and selling to a different audience. Your recruitment video needs to show people what it's like to work at your company, rather than what it's like to buy your products or services.

Employer branding is a whole specialist area, and some companies will have a completely separate website for recruitment. The messaging needs to be slightly different, so having a specific recruitment video is key.

That said, if budget won't allow it, you can still use all your other marketing videos and assets when recruiting. I exhibited at a careers fair recently and was amazed to be the only business showing a video. Of course, I need to have video playing to demonstrate what we do, but the other companies could have easily had their marketing videos playing on a screen to help sell the idea of working for them.

OFFICE/FACILITY TOUR

An Office/Facility Tour is a great way to show behind the scenes. It's particularly good if you've invested in your facility recently. If you've just built a new factory, had your office refurbished or moved premises, this is a great time to make a tour video.

There are a few different ways to make a tour video. They can be a literal fly-through using an FPV drone – a small drone that's piloted via goggles. These can look really cool if done well. The famous one is the bowling alley drone video – look it up if you haven't seen it. The key to these videos is the planning and choreography.

But you don't have to use an FPV drone. You can showcase your premises using more traditional ground-based filming methods. A walkthrough with a camera on a gimbal can (and should) look super-smooth. You could have a presenter or Voiceover for these videos, or you may use motion graphics on screen to talk about the different areas of your site.

Either way, showing off your premises demonstrates your facility, your capacity and how well you look after your people. All of this helps build more trust with potential customers.

INNOVATION VIDEO

An Innovation Video is an example of documenting something in your business, demonstrating what you're doing and how forward-thinking you are. It doesn't have to be innovation; it could be investments in other areas. The point is you're proving how you're moving forward and investing in ways to improve your services or products.

Again, these could be interviews with management or relevant employees, a presenter, voiceover or text graphics.

Demonstrating how you're investing in your business helps build trust. Everyone wants to work with successful people and innovation is a key part of your success. It's the reason you're a market leader today and the reason you'll still be at the forefront of your industry in ten years.

This is a great example of documenting things which you may think of as 'normal' but can become a really powerful piece of marketing content.

MEET THE TEAM VIDEO

You probably already have a Meet the Team or About page on your website with headshots of the team. The reason you have this is to build trust with potential customers. You're showing who works there, how friendly they all are and the expertise you have within the business.

You can take this to the next level with a meet-the-team video. The options for how to do this are endless! It could be interviews with funny outtakes, you could film the team on an away day, or down the pub after work. Or it might simply be clips of them at work with some information about each person next to them. You can get creative here and make a video your employees will be proud of, whilst showing potential customers why you're the right choice for them.

SERVICE VIDEOS

Service videos show your customers how to service the product they've bought from you. You're taking them step by step through the process, showing which tools and service pack they'll need.

You're adding a lot of value to your existing customers, building brand reputation and loyalty. You can also use these videos in your marketing, demonstrating how you look after your customers.

As discussed earlier, service videos also benefit your customer service team. They'll receive fewer calls from customers asking how to service the product. When they do get those questions, they have this resource to direct them to.

As well as helping your customers, it's also an opportunity to demonstrate your expertise and produce a piece of content that adds to your brand. As such, it needs to show your business in a professional light. A quick phone video may do the trick in terms of communicating how to service the product, but a high-quality video will improve people's perception of your brand.

ASSEMBLY VIDEOS

Assembly videos are similar to service videos in terms of the benefits they bring to your marketing and customer service team.

Rather than showing how to service the product, the assembly video shows how to (you've guessed it) assemble the product. Again, you're demonstrating how well you look after your customers, building brand loyalty with existing customers and attracting new ones.

This is also an opportunity to address buyer's remorse. Buyer's remorse is something that occurs just after the sale when people can feel worried about whether they've made the right decision. They've committed to buying from you and spent the money, but they're not yet sure whether they've made the right decision.

If you can quickly direct them to an assembly video, you help them at this critical stage. You're adding value by ensuring they get the product assembled and into use as soon as possible. In doing so, you provide the reassurance they need.

Think about the entire process from when they receive the product to having it all set up and working. You want to make this as smooth as possible. You could do this by providing a QR code in the user manual which takes them to the assembly video. The assembly video then congratulates them for their purchase and takes them through the assembly and set-up process. Depending on your product and brand, it can be a good opportunity to inject a little humour at this stage too.

ONBOARDING VIDEO

If you're a service business, your version of an assembly video is an onboarding/what's next video. Again, this is addressing the buyer's remorse phase and helping your customer get set up. The onboarding video guides your new customer through the process now they've decided to work with you.

If you're going to provide a service to them, you can talk through the next steps, showing them what to expect, what's needed from them and what you'll be providing. You see these videos a lot with SaaS (Software as a Service) businesses. When you sign up for a software platform, you usually have a short trial period. It's their job to get you using the software, so you make the most of the trial period and get to see all the great advantages of using it. To do this, they take you through the setup process and guide you step by step into making the most of their platform.

This can be delivered as an email sequence to your new customers or triggered by certain events. For example, when they pay their booking deposit invoice or sign your terms and conditions.

As with all your marketing videos, this is a chance to inject some brand personality and reinforce your values. You have the chance here to really impress your new customers, making them feel they've made the right decision in choosing to work with you. This is the time when they're excited about their decision and most likely to make a referral.

FAQ VIDEOS

Service videos, assembly videos and onboarding videos help your customers by addressing their questions and showing them how to assemble or service their product. This approach can be extended to answer *all* your customers' (and potential customers') questions.

Make a list of the questions you get asked regularly. You can prioritise these in order of popularity, then begin making videos to answer these questions and post them on the FAQ or customer services page of your website.

As mentioned earlier, if you're in marketing and making FAQ videos – make sure you ask for budget from customer services because these videos are really going to benefit them too!

FAQ videos can also help your SEO, as discussed earlier. The questions your customers are asking directly are probably being asked by others on the internet. By answering these questions, you're providing a valuable resource. If people find their way to your website when they search for answers, the search engines will be more likely to point others to your FAQ page too. Once they arrive here, they'll see you offer the service they're looking for and may convert into customers as a result.

FAQ videos posted to social media will also help raise your profile as an expert and thought leader in your sector. We discussed making these types of social media videos earlier. The polished high-production value versions of these will have an even greater impact, as people see you in the very best light (literally). You can even use the quick social media versions as a testing ground to help you decide which ones to make into high-quality video assets – testing people's responses and your messaging.

LOBBY VIDEOS

If you have a lobby area where customers come and wait at your premises, there's an opportunity to have a video playing to reinforce your brand.

You could have a meet-the-team style video or a showcase of the services you offer. This might be similar to your home-page video, taking the viewer on a journey through every-thing you do and showing your business in the best light.

Like a homepage video, you wouldn't normally have any sound in this type of lobby video – otherwise, on loop, it could get irritating for your waiting customers (and your receptionist!).

If you don't have a specific lobby video, consider using one of your other marketing videos here. Take advantage of this space, while you have your customer's attention for a short while. If they've come in to speak to you about service A, the video could also showcase services B, C & D, which they didn't realise you offered. In other words, you can gently upsell your range of services at this point.

CHALLENGE VIDEOS

Challenge videos are a showcase of what your product can do by setting a challenge and demonstrating the product taking on the challenge – and of course, completing it!

For example, can this chainsaw cut through a large diameter tree in a certain amount of time? Or can a certain tool complete an intricate job to a high standard? Think about what your customers are using the product for and what might impress them, then set yourself the challenge of completing that task.

When you post a video like this on YouTube, you can use an enticing title and thumbnail image to draw people in – I'm sure you've seen these in your feed on YouTube, clicking on it to find out what it's all about. I'm not suggesting clickbait here – a title that's overdramatic and not totally relevant to the video – you have to deliver what you promise. But you can still make it exciting and draw people into watching your video.

EVENT VIDEOS

Event videos speak for themselves; you're showcasing an event you hosted. This serves two purposes; to show people who weren't there what they missed so they'll sign up next time, and to keep those who were there excited about the event afterwards – sharing it on social media and with colleagues.

The speed with which you get the video out there after the event can be a huge advantage and often overlooked. James Ashford talks about this in relation to event videos. He would ensure his event round-up videos were posted a couple of hours after the event finished, so people on their journeys back would see and share them while the excitement was still there. The danger of taking too long to publish an event video is that people have moved on to the next thing and are less likely to share or comment on your video.

It was a fast-turnaround event video that led to a friendship with Matt Chilton of Zenoot.com who wrote the Foreword for this book. I brought one of our videographers along to the MACH show (an industry trade show for manufacturers here in the UK). We filmed in the morning all around the exhibition, edited the video in the afternoon, and released it on LinkedIn before leaving the show. The video caught the attention of Matt, a manufacturing marketing expert with clients across the sector, and a fantastic industry news platform. We've formed a working friendship, having regular calls to discuss the industry and see where we can help one another. This is leading to referrals and work for both of us.

That said, your event videos will be used to promote the next event, so you could consider having two versions. One which comes out quickly and maybe isn't as polished, and another which comes out later to advertise the next event you'll be putting on.

Either way, your event videos want to be snappy, fast-paced, and interesting. Unless you're showcasing one very specific part of the show, in which case you might have a presenter talking about it, you'll want to cover all the key points of interest in a short space of time. Make sure your production crew know when things are happening and what is likely to be of most interest so they can be there to film at the right time.

BUILD VIDEOS

If you're building new premises, extending an old one or installing new equipment, showcase this with a video of the build.

This could take various formats; a popular thing to do is a time-lapse of the build, installing a camera for the entire process which takes a photo every few minutes. Time-lapse videos can be quite captivating. We've all stopped to watch something happening in time-lapse before – it's cool to see a building going up at high speed for example. There are companies that specialise in time-lapse capture and have kit they install and monitor remotely. Alternatively, you might buy a small time-lapse camera to install and monitor yourself.

You can also showcase different aspects of the build as it progresses. You might film a presenter showing us around or interviewing members of the team. These videos could be released periodically throughout the project and then combined into a final overview video to have on your website.

Drones can also be used for a build video, depending on the scale and location of your premises. While you couldn't leave a drone up for more than about 30-40 minutes due to battery life, if there was a significant event happening, you could capture that from the perspective of a drone to make an eye-catching video.

Make the most of whatever's going on in your business by documenting the process and talking about it on your social channels. Get people involved in the process and they'll be more bought into your brand as a result.

TRAINING VIDEOS

You can use videos to help train staff. This could be a stand-alone training video that requires no other explanation, or it could form part of an in-person training session.

Either way, a training video can do two things. Firstly, the video should, of course, get the message across and make sure it's understood. We've all seen those very plain, boring, and monotonous training videos made in the 70's, with someone talking slowly to the camera about...who knows. We've switched off by then!

To get the message across, your training videos need to be engaging and stand out. You can tell a story, inject some humour, or take people on a journey – either way, it needs to be compelling just like a marketing video. You're marketing the message to your people.

Secondly, this is a chance to build loyalty and motivation with your staff. They want to feel proud of the company they work for and seeing a high-end training video can help. Show them you care about their safety or development by investing in a decent, high-quality, engaging video. You may also be showing them other areas of the company, so you want it to look its very best to make them feel excited and proud to work there.

MINI DOCUMENTARIES

Documentaries tell a story. They bring the viewer on board and into the lives of people whose story you're telling. They bring real connection between the viewer and the subject. They don't always have to be huge-scale projects; you can make a very short video in the style of a documentary.

Making a short documentary about your business, or an aspect of your business, like innovation for example, is a great way to showcase your people, products and services authentically. You can bring in other people too, like customers, to tell their stories and hear how they've benefited from working with you. This can be done in a 3-5 minute mini-documentary, where we interview key people in the business and show what goes on behind the scenes.

These documentaries don't *have* to be short. If you have a great story to tell (which everyone does, without exception), a longer documentary can form a fantastic piece of cornerstone content. It could tell the story of the founder, how and why they got started, or it could be focused on the process of carrying out the work you do.

However, the best documentaries will do both at the same time. While we learn about your process, there should be personal stories woven in. This brings the human connection to what you do, building that all-important trust factor.

It's important to follow the GREAT principles here. It could be easy to create a documentary that comes across as an advert for your business. You have to make sure you're giving something, adding value and educating the viewer – genuinely. Trust that in doing so, you will buy people into your brand.

There are examples of longer-format documentaries working extremely well for businesses. Imagine your ideal customer wanting to sit down in the evening and watch a documentary about your business. This can only happen if you're genuinely adding value and providing a great experience with the film you make. But it can happen.

And if people are willing to spend 30-40 minutes of their lives watching a film about your business because they find it fascinating, there's a very good chance they're going to become a customer one day.

SOCIAL SNIPPETS

As with all the content you create, make the most of it by extracting social media-friendly snippets. These might simply be a section of the main video, or you might ask your production company to make short custom edits from each part of the video, talking about different subjects.

These could be used as trailers, teasing the main video and directing people to come and watch over on your website.

Whatever type of video assets you create, maximise your investment by making these short-form social snippets from them.

As mentioned before, film yourself making the content. If you have a production crew filming with you, make the most of that event by filming them filming you! Make behind-the-scenes videos whilst the production is in progress and tag everyone involved. Bring your audience into the process and they'll feel part of your brand.

Launching a video with some build-up can help immensely – tell people it's coming, show them behind the scenes of filming and tease it in. It gets people bought into your brand and excited to see the final video.

BONUS BENEFIT

One of the hidden bonuses in producing stunning videos of your product, company and brand, is that of motivating your employees. They may work in the factory producing hundreds of products every day and as with everyone else, become used to seeing them. Or they may work in another area of the business, part of a larger team bringing your product or service to your customers.

Seeing their work, your team and your happy customers in a beautiful video can help motivate them, making all those hours worthwhile.

I like this story:

There was once a team of stone masons working away, cutting and moving big heavy stones every day in the hot sun. They'd be heaving stones into position, lugging them up and down ladders and making very slow progress, one stone at a time. One of the workers looked very tired, beaten down by the weight of his work. When asked what he was doing, he replied "I'm cutting this stone into shape and taking it over there to put on top of the others". Another worker seemed almost to be walking on air, he was so happy and enthused by his work. When asked the same question, his eyes lit up, he looked to the sky and replied "I'm building a cathedral".

This story is usually told in the context of leadership. If your people know what they're working towards, they'll be on board with the mission, and everyone will work together.

The cornerstone content (no pun intended here!) you invest in will not only help market your business to potential customers, but it will also motivate your employees by showing their work looking amazing and what a great team they work with. They'll feel proud to be part of your organisation and more like the second stone mason in the story.

One of the best compliments we receive as a video production company is to hear that the factory, product or process looks so much better in the video than in real life. Often this is a case of us having looked at it with a fresh pair of eyes and spotted things that everyone else takes for granted, but which in fact, are incredible things happening every day.

GETTING STARTED

If you're creating your first video marketing assets or looking to refresh your existing videos, my suggestion is to start with the following videos, in the following order:

1. Testimonial Videos
2. Product Videos
3. Brand Video

Testimonial videos can be relatively straightforward to make and pack a punch when it comes to ROI (Return on Investment). Other people telling your potential customers about the benefit you've brought to them is extremely powerful.

Product videos take things to the next level, demonstrating your product/service and the benefits and outcomes you deliver, which is backed up by the testimonial videos you already have. A well-produced video will make your product or service look fantastic.

Finally, the brand video brings everything together, telling the story behind the brand, showing what you stand for, why you exist and how you benefit your customers. People can then go to the product video to find out more about the product, and the testimonial videos to gain trust in you and your business.

Producing your first set of video assets in this order will allow you to build your experience in making videos, as well as your library of assets. The testimonial videos help you understand what your customers are saying, which is useful when it comes to scripting the product and brand videos. You can use what they've said to help describe your products or services in the product videos. The Brand Video is the most complex video to script and produce, bringing together everything your business is about. You can even use the footage from the testimonial and product videos in the brand video.

Remember, you can also create social media snippets from these videos, meaning you'll have a library of content to use.

Whether you're a marketing manager, head of marketing, sales director or owner of the business, this suite of videos will make a huge difference. Having these assets will mean you have high-impact, quality content to draw on for several years to come.

I like to think of video as being a tool in your toolbox. Once you've put the work and investment into creating the video, you can pull it out and use it as needed, to create the business outcomes you want to achieve.

CHAPTER SUMMARY

There are many types of cornerstone video marketing assets you can create, and hopefully you now have some inspiration for videos you hadn't considered previously.

Make an initial list of which videos you think will benefit your business most and you can work through them over time. Consider trying some ideas yourself first before you bring in a production company.

Whoever you choose to work with on these videos will be able to advise on the best approach to take. This includes both the messaging, style and best way to capture your business on film.

I suggest starting with testimonial videos, moving to product videos and then onto a company/brand video. This will provide you with a fantastic suite of video assets to use for several years.

CHAPTER 9
BECOME THE GREATEST

We've talked about how to create exceptional content using the 5 principles of GREAT. Now we need to put that into practice and take some steps to make you the GREATEST.

To do that, we need to add the E, S & T.

These additional pointers will help you become consistent and achieve the best results from your video marketing. Consistency is the key to success - we all know that and many of us struggle with it. This book is getting written by being consistent; I'm getting up early every morning to put in some writing time. I won't get it all done in a day, but over time, by being consistent, I will.

Consistency builds trust. It's all about showing up every day to add value to your audience with a consistent message.

So, let's add the final three letters to see how to become the GREATEST:

GIVE - to your audience

RECORD - and document your journey/process

EDUCATE - your followers

ADD VALUE - at all times

TARGET - your message towards your ideal customer and the outcome you want

ESTABLISH A HABIT - consistency through habits

SYSTEMISE - make it simple for yourself to create and post content

TEST - finally, assess your posts and content on a continual basis

We'll look at the E, S and T in more detail now.

ESTABLISH A HABIT

Many people either can't get started with creating video marketing content or when they do, they can't keep going. They'll start one week, have a great run of 3 or 4 posts, then go off it and drop down to zero again. I know how this goes from personal experience.

We know marketing should be at the forefront of our minds. It's arguably the most important business function. People have to know we exist before they can even contemplate buying from us.

Establishing a habit of producing content is super important. A good place to understand more about the power of habits is James Clear's book, Atomic Habits.

Atomic means small (but powerful) in this case. He argues that by creating small habits in our lives, we can have a huge impact. The regularity and consistency of the habit means things get done.

For many of us, producing marketing content and posting to social media is not something that comes naturally. It's not our first thought in any given situation. We miss opportunities to post about things that happen in our business all the time. How many times have you come away from something and thought "Ahh, I should've posted about that!". It's not because we don't know how to, it's because we're not in the habit of doing so.

Personally, I find it much easier to get into the habit of doing something when I enjoy doing it. The irony is, I enjoy doing things when I do them regularly. It all comes back to getting started - we need to start this cycle of regularity to begin enjoying it and therefore get into a habit.

When I start a habit, I like to keep the bar low. There's no point trying to run a marathon every day, you'll get burned out immediately. You'd start by running a quarter of a mile each day and building it from there (this doesn't constitute marathon running advice by the way!).

It's the same with creating content. What's the simplest way you can get started?

Depending on what resources you have, it's unlikely you'll have access to a full production crew to film and produce your content regularly. It would be lovely to make a high-end video every day, but to start with at least, it may not be realistic. Sure, there are people who do this - the Gary Vaynerchuks and Steven Bartletts of the world. But they have a huge team behind them, helping to plan, produce and post the content.

However, everyone starts somewhere and even those guys started small. I do it myself too - arguably I have access to a production crew regularly (my team), but most of the time it's unrealistic to get them to produce my social media content because they have client work to focus on. The important thing is getting something out there, with a good clear message.

So, the phone often comes out and I hit record. I get the message out there and keep my content flowing. Don't get hung up on the technicalities and think everything has to be produced to a high standard - if you have a message to get out there, sometimes the most important thing you can do is:

get the message out there. In whatever form you can manage that day.

How often should you be doing this? Well, there are two objectives here; one is to get content out regularly and the other is to establish the habit of producing content, so you don't miss opportunities.

I've tried many different approaches to this, posting 3 times a week, making content once a month and scheduling it, posting daily etc. There's no right or wrong answer, you need an approach that works for you. For me, if I want to build a solid habit, I have to go in daily.

It's like giving up sugar - I'm all or nothing. Deciding to eat a little bit less sugar doesn't really work for me. A little bit creeps up to a little bit more and so on. The same with taking days off posting to social media, one day off leads to another day off, then another and so on until I'm back to doing nothing. Does this sound familiar to you?

Now, I'm not suggesting you post every day for the rest of your life, because I know it will put you off. But, challenging yourself to a sustained period of posting something every day will help build the habit of making content. Once the habit is formed, you'll find it much easier to continue producing regular content, because it will be on your mind.

Estimates vary for how long it takes to form a habit. Some people say 30 days, others 90. Personally, I think 30 days is not long enough. I need longer to properly establish a habit. I'd recommend 60-90 days. Or 100 days if you like round numbers!

Once you've established this habit, it's going to change your thinking. When there's a new delivery to the factory, for example, you'll see this as an opportunity to make a video. When you have a meeting on innovation plans over the next 12 months, you'll see an opportunity here.

Because you're challenging yourself to produce a daily video, you'll be looking for opportunities. Start a list of content ideas, so if you haven't found an opportunity that day, you can simply pick something from your list.

Once you're in the habit of producing regular social media videos, you'll soon spot opportunities for getting a production company in to make high-end videos to really boost your brand and marketing.

SYSTEMISE

Having systems in place for making content is another way to make sure it gets done. If it's easy and you know what you're doing, you're a lot more likely to actually do it. When all you have to do is walk over to your set-up, hit record, and deliver your lines, you'll do it every day.

To quote James Clear in Atomic Habits again, he says:

> "You do not rise to the level of your goals, you fall to the level of your systems."

In other words, it's great to have a goal of putting out a video on social media several times a week, but you need to have a system in place to make this happen. Otherwise, if it's difficult to do, it simply won't happen.

So how can you systemise your approach to making social media videos?

Firstly, you need to know how you're going to do it. Are you going to record on your phone using the phone camera app? Or is there another app you'll use for some reason? Are you going to bring in a production crew to regularly create a batch of high-quality video content?

Note for LinkedIn users: at the time of writing, I find the camera app built into LinkedIn produces very bad-looking videos. I guess it's compressing the file differently. My suggestion is to record using your phone camera app or a third-party app, rather than using the camera option within LinkedIn.

For making social media videos on the fly, my current work-flow is this:

1. Record to my phone using the camera app and an external microphone
2. Import to a third-party app to add captions and trim the beginning and end, if needed
3. Export back to my photo/video album
4. Start my LinkedIn post with selected video
5. Write my text
6. Copy/paste hashtags from the Notes app

This workflow keeps things simple. I can do it easily whilst on a shoot or travelling (as a passenger - don't do this while driving, obvs!).

The second step where we trim the beginning and end is quite important. No one wants to sit there watching as you fumble for the record button! You can easily trim these parts out. Or even better, get practised at hitting record while looking at the camera and start talking as soon as the recording starts.

Another side note here: you can start and stop recording on most phones using the volume button. This means, that if you're holding the phone in your hand, you can start/stop with that hand easily, without having to jolt the phone by using the screen button.

Copy/pasting the hashtags into the post is another way to simplify your process. Currently, on LinkedIn it's a bit of a pain to get the # symbol - it used to be there for you on the phone app, but it's more hidden now. I mean, these are first-world problems of course - in the grand scheme of things, it's not a big deal! But I find that keeping a list of hashtags on my notes app makes it easier. I simply open the note, select the group of hashtags I want to use, copy, and then paste into the end of my post.

Keep your system simple, then build on it as you get into the habit. If you want to add extras, you can do this as you go, but I highly recommend having a simple system to start with, one you can do quickly and easily. The objective here is to get your GREAT content out there, regularly.

When it comes to recording a video on your phone, another way to make it easy for yourself is to have a dedicated space for making them. Can you set up a phone holder on your desk, in your office or factory? The main aim is to make it easy for yourself, so it happens.

When you look at the Gary Vaynerchuks and Steven Bartletts of the world, they have a team of people who take care of everything to do with the editing and uploading. They can make and post multiple pieces of content, produced to a high standard, each day. However, some of them will still make a quick video on their phones to get a message out there. Just yesterday I watched Grant Cardone (billionaire property investor and educator) delivering a message from a swimming pool. Terrible audio quality and camera moving around everywhere (admittedly a nice setting with palm trees!), but I still listened because I was interested in the message.

Think about which elements of this you could outsource to make it simple and ensure it happens. Perhaps you have an assistant who can post to your business page after you've recorded the content.

The other part of the systemising process to mention is reusing content for other platforms. As I said earlier, I think you should focus your efforts on one platform to begin with and not get overwhelmed. However, at some point, you'll want to start posting to multiple platforms at once. I suggest having a robust system in place for managing your content and making sure it all gets posted everywhere you want it to.

You'll probably want to tweak the message for different platforms, as they each have different audiences. I suggest posting to one platform one day, and then flowing it down to the other platform(s) during the following days.

Again, the main objective here is to get your message out there. Make your system for creating and posting content as simple as possible so that it happens.

Once you have a system in place for producing social media content, you can move on to making high-quality video assets. Although more complex, you'll be able to create a system for this. It will likely involve bringing in a production company to help. Part of your process might be an ongoing relationship with a team you trust and enjoy working with.

Our regular clients will call us up each time they have some content to create. We know how they work, and they know our process. We'll work through the ideas and begin to generate concepts for their next set of video assets.

Simplify your ideas and make it happen. If you want to produce a range of product videos, create a system that works for you - a structure for the video that can be repeated for each product, whilst still looking amazing. Your production company will be able to help with this - explain how you'd like to systemise things and ask them to produce a plan that can be repeated.

With a solid system in place, you'll soon become the GREATEST at making content to help build your brand.

TEST

Testing is an ongoing and necessary process once we start putting content out. It might be as simple as asking people what they like about your content (remember to ask the right people - your target market) or keeping a record of how many impressions, likes and comments you get. Or it might be more in-depth, involving split testing different styles and approaches.

Either way, it's important to test different types of content and take note of what your audience resonates with. Having a regular content creation schedule (E and S) means you'll have data to work with. If you only post once a month, there's not much to go on; it's hard to tell whether the content you posted was good, or you just got lucky.

By posting regularly, you can see trends and get a feel for what's working and what's not. But don't be put off by thinking you have to record all your statistics every single day. Remember, we're not building blockers and excuses for creating content here, we're trying to get you making and posting content more regularly.

Once a month perhaps, go through your posts and create a spreadsheet of the key metrics (again, don't be put off by this - I like spreadsheets, but not everyone does - use a system that works for you). These could include all or some of the following:

- Description of the post (I just copy/paste the words from the post)
- The type of post (photo, video, talking to camera, behind the scenes etc.)

- Which day it was posted
- Time of day you posted
- Whether you used captions and if so, what style
- Hashtags used in the post
- Number of likes
- Number of comments
- Number of impressions (how many people saw the post)

You'll begin to build a good picture of what your audience likes to hear from you.

A quick note on this; I'm not suggesting you pander to your audience just to get likes and comments. That won't work - you'll hate it, it won't seem genuine and gradually no one will listen. Although we're looking at what works, your content must remain authentic and follow the GREAT approach to have the most engagement.

Testing is about trying different approaches, looking at the data to see what's working, and creating more content with that in mind.

This final part of the GREATEST approach is ongoing. You now know how to create GREAT content. The best people follow this approach and then continue to test, re-evaluate and tweak. It's a loop and hopefully, by following the advice in this book, you'll begin to enjoy the process and make it part of your everyday work. It may even feel more like play than work!

CHAPTER SUMMARY

- Consistency builds trust – show up regularly for your audience.
- Establishing a habit ensures you'll carry on creating marketing content in the long-run.
- Set the bar low to build the habit.
- Focus on building the habit over a sustained period – I suggest at least 90 days.
- Create a system for making and posting content – keep it simple so that it gets done.
- You fall to the level of your systems, so make sure they're robust and easy to follow.
- Test what's working for you by tracking progress.
- Evaluate it on a regular basis and fine-tune your content.
- Don't pander to your audience, stay authentic but do what works.

CHAPTER 10
YOU'VE GOT THIS

Generating ideas for marketing content is a challenge for any business. The principles we've discussed in this book apply across the board.

Consistently posting useful, helpful, and genuine content will go a long way to building trust with potential and existing customers. Coming up with ideas is easier than you think - you have everything you need already. If you've become used to what you do every day and see it as normal or mundane, you just need to look at it through a different lens.

Make a start and more ideas will come, they'll begin to flow. Keep a note of your ideas, then when it's time to post or create a new marketing video, you'll have a list at the ready.

By taking this approach, you'll see your business in a new light and rediscover everything that interested you in the first place. If you're sold on what you do, you're in a better position to sell it to others.

This is your chance to tell the world about something you love, share your passion, and help people by letting them know about what you offer.

Go create.

AUTHOR'S NOTES

I hope I've encouraged you to either start creating your first videos or to improve your strategy and discover effective ways to use video throughout your business.

I'd wanted to write a book for a while, but the concepts hadn't felt quite right until now. As I've talked about in this book, it needed to add value to people. It's only with *time* that the ideas have been able to develop – through conversations with clients and people I've advised.

Writing this book has taught me a degree of patience. I have to admit, when I have an idea, I prefer to get it done quickly! But writing, more than most other things, has taught me that adding one brick at a time will get the wall built. Doing a little bit each day adds up to a lot. I like to think of it as pushing the needle forward. If I keep doing a little towards it, over time the needle will get to where it needs to be.

Writing is a great reminder of the importance of reviewing your work. During one of the final read-throughs before sending out the draft to people, I cut 2000 words – that's 5% of the book! Although I just wanted to get it out there, Poppy (thankfully) convinced me to take my time, go through it again and be ruthless.

It's like engineering in many ways; cutting out the unnecessary words to make the text as efficient as possible.

I've been using a writing program called Scrivener, and I'm now a huge fan! It allows you to see all your chapters easily and make notes inside the chapters as you go along. I'm a big advocate of having the right tools for the job, and I've found this to be perfect for writing long-form content. Thank you to fellow mastermind member Kent Sanders for the recommendation.

I write best first thing in the morning. I've read books and heard many things about morning routines – exercise, journaling, meditating etc. But I've found that for me, the best way to start my day is to get out of bed and immediately onto my laptop to write for 1-2 hours.

Crucially, I don't turn on my phone and avoid looking at emails, social media etc. so that I've got a clear head for writing. I've tried writing later in the day, but once my head is full of other work, it hasn't been so effective.

The best time of day will differ for everyone of course; it's about finding what works best for you and protecting that time. My wife and children have been amazingly supportive, enabling and encouraging me to carry on.

However you choose to implement the advice in this book, my main objective is for you to succeed and live the life you want. That may sound unconnected to making marketing videos, but I firmly believe that by improving your business (as an employee, director, CEO or owner) you will improve your whole life.

Remember, a rising tide lifts all boats – if you've found this book helpful, share it, lend it, give it and recommend it to others.

Tag me on your videos, I'd love to see what you create and how it benefits your business!

ACKNOWLEDGMENTS

Firstly, I wouldn't be doing work I love, let alone have written a book, if it wasn't for the endless support of my wife, Poppy. Thank you for your belief in me and your patience while I changed careers and now, while I'm building a business. Thank you for embracing the extra-early morning alarm call while I wrote this book and for all your helpful advice and feedback. I love you very much.

My children have been amazing too – encouraging me and supporting me along the way. Just now, in fact, Isabel came in and said how 'cool' it was that someone had written a Foreword for me! Bel, Rose, Frank, Patience and Jemima - you're all such an inspiration every day, and I love having a house full of happy, laughing children.

On the subject of the foreword, thank you Matt for not only writing that but for reading the whole book and giving me such helpful feedback. I really enjoy our regular phone calls and hearing your positive insights on the manufacturing industry. I look forward to working together more in the future.

Mum and Dad – thank you. You're always there supporting whatever I do, even though it must be worrying at times!

When I thought about the book cover design, there was only one person I wanted to ask; Ian Woodley. Specialising in the industrial sector, you knew how this book needed to look. I'm constantly amazed at how designers can turn a blank page into a stunning piece of practical artwork! Thanks for all your support and collaboration over the years.

Vincent Pugliese has been a huge inspiration and support over the last 6 years, as my coach and mentor. We've still never met in person, but I feel like we're kindred spirits and great friends. Thank you for believing in me.

Harry O'Connor – you've been there since the early days and strongly encouraged me to start making videos. Thank you for all your support.

Tom and Tom – you're such fantastic team members, every day I feel like I've landed on my feet finding you guys to work with. Your dedication to building a successful business is inspiring. Thank you.

Several people have given their time to read through the first draft and provide me with excellent feedback, for which I'm extremely grateful! In no particular order:

Jon Johnson – thank you for all your support, our regular catch-ups are always inspiring. Thank you for commenting on my LinkedIn post all those years ago, and generously speaking to me on the phone.

Gary Howell – we've only met once I think, but I always appreciate your honest and helpful feedback on the content I put out there.

Peter Redstone – my uncle. You've been a continuous source of inspiration throughout my life, maybe more than you know. Your positivity and enthusiasm are infectious!

Stuart Rose – thank you for all your support over the years, We met when we were in the early stages of video production and seemed to just click (no pun intended!). I always enjoy catching up and hearing what's going on in your world.

Xander Freeman – you've been here for more of the industrial niche journey than you might realise, as one of my first 'proper' clients in that sector. Thanks for believing in me and giving me the opportunity, it was confirmation that I was on the right track.

Jenny South – thank you for such detailed and honest feedback on the draft. You've been a fan of our work, very encouraging and supportive since you found us online. It's always fun to work with you and your team on projects.

Richard Snell – my father-in-law; I feel very fortunate to have such great in-laws. You and Suzy are the best!

Greg McQueen – thank you for the helpful feedback on the draft and your continued support, it's much appreciated.

Finally – to all our clients over the years and going forward, we wouldn't have a business without you. Thank you for trusting us to deliver your content. I love seeing you all grow and I'm proud to have contributed, even if only in a small way, to your success.

ABOUT THE AUTHOR

Dan Barker is a former aerospace engineer who became a full-time pro-photographer in 2018. His specialism is industrial, where he combines his engineering experience with photography and video know-how to create marketing content that stands out and efficiently communicates his clients' value to their customers.

The business has grown, and his team now produce high-end videos for industrial businesses up and down the country.

He's on a mission to eliminate dull marketing and help elevate UK manufacturing.

Contact Dan:

dan@danbarkerstudios.com

www.danbarkerstudios.com

www.youtube.com/@DanBarkerOfficial

www.linkedin.com/in/danbarkerstudios/

Printed in Great Britain
by Amazon